ENDORSEMENT

"I met Wade at a YPO event in 2004. He applied the principles from my seminar to build a multi-million dollar business. He has also helped dozens of entrepreneurs take their businesses to the next level. This book expands the reach of his business coaching, and it's a must-read book for every entrepreneur. *Wake-Up Call* is an excellent addition to the Scaling Up family of books."

- **Verne Harnish**, Founder Entrepreneurs' Organization (EO) and author of *Scaling Up (Rockefeller Habits 2.0)*

"Wade Wyant, in his book *Wake-Up Call,* provides business owners with bite-sized business vitamins, which wrestle down the many nagging ailments we all encounter in building a successful business. This book should be read regularly by all on your leadership team. Then take action!"

Jack Daly, Serial entrepreneur, CEO coach, professional sales speaker and author of *Hyper Growth*

"I wasn't sleeping well, and I needed wisdom. Then, thank God, the clear and short chapters in *Wake-Up Call* gave me exactly what I longed for. Clarity replaced uncertainty, my partnership problems became win-wins, and my business was transformed. If you want success — and great sleep — these pages are for you."

- **Tyler Durman**, Best-selling author of *Counterintuitive: Bite-Sized Wisdom for Parents and Teachers*. President, Hope For Parents.

"*Wake-Up Call* will change the way you run your business. I wish I had read this book before starting mine. Thank you, Wade, for sharing your valuable insights. This book is a game changer!"

- **Ken Fortier**, Author of *NetPlus Connections*

"Real life, down to earth, practical business advice that every entrepreneur needs to learn and relearn again and again."

- **George Moss**, Recording Artist/Entrepreneur

"What impresses me most about Wade is his transparency, embracing failures and setbacks as *the* catalyst for success. I don't need a coach who helps me in the good times; I need a coach who can run with me through the inevitable storms, uncertainty, and doubt that surround business in this exponential age. Wade is an exceptional coach because he has walked a mile in our shoes! This is your Wake-Up Call, so embrace it! "

- **John D. Anderson**, Founder of the Detroit EO Chapter and author of *Replace Retirement: Living your Legacy in the Exponential Age*

"I was introduced to Wade at an Inc. 5000 event 8 years ago, and he is a person/businessperson I admire. I have watched his entrepreneurial journey from founder, to operator, to consultant, to author and back again to founder. Seeing what Wade has built each step of the way in a selfless people-focused manner gives him a unique perspective on business building, culture, and life. Anyone that reads this book has the opportunity to gain from his insight. These insights can be instantly applied to their own businesses and lives. Get ready for your personal Wake-Up Call!"

- **Matt Jung**, Co-Founder Comfort Research, Founder Orange Dot Ventures, Business Innovator and Culture Evangelist

WAKE-UP CALL

WAKE-UP CALL

WADE W. WYANT

Edited by
MELISSA MAIN
&
TRUDY CORDLE

Title: Wake-up call: insights for entrepreneurs to have more freedom, reduce drama, and scale their businesses / Wade W. Wyant; edited by Melissa Main; illustrated by Leah Buchanan.

Description: Includes bibliographical references. | Grand Rapids, MI: Jaatoo, 2021.

Identifiers: LCCN: 2021919186 | ISBN: 978-1-7371229-0-6 (print) | 978-1-7371229-1-3 (ebook)

Subjects: LCSH Entrepreneurship. | Success in business. | Leadership. | Management. | Work-life balance. | Small business. | BISAC BUSINESS & ECONOMICS / Mentoring & Coaching | BUSINESS & ECONOMICS / Entrepreneurship | BUSINESS & ECONOMICS / Leadership

Classification: LCC HF5386 .W93 2022| DDC 658.4/09--dc23

For my wife, Alicia, and our kids
(Ethan, Elijah, Ian and Elora) — my first wake-up call.

CONTENTS

PART III
EXECUTION

PART IV
SALES/CASH

PREFACE

I failed in my first two businesses, but with my third business, my company became a six-time Inc. 5000 winner. What changed my ability to have success? I started listening to wake-up calls.

Many times in my life, I had a wake-up call come in the form of advice, an observation, or a book I had read. Learning from other people's mistakes also gave me wake-up calls. When I acted on those wake-up calls, I had success. Other times, I didn't listen. Maybe it was because of laziness, logistics, or timing issues. Looking back, I wish I had listened to all those wake-up calls.

As you are reading this book, I want you to remember something I tell all of my clients: "I am not your boss." At the beginning of any class I teach or in any advisory or consulting work that I do, I always start out by saying, "I am not your boss." I have the people repeat, "Wade is not my boss." The reason I do that is because I am going to flood them with many ideas and concepts, but that doesn't mean that they should implement all those things. They are things that I believe, and things that I have used in my business. However, the ideas and concepts that I tell them may not be right for them. As you read this book, I want you to start by saying aloud, "Wade is not my boss."

———

My goal with this book is to say, "Here's what I've learned along the way." I want to fill in some of the cracks for you, so that you can have a smoother journey. If some of these wake-up calls resonate with you and help you along your way, then I've done my job.

My main goal in the paragraph above is to challenge entrepreneurs, but my second goal (and perhaps where the book can have the biggest impact) is to open up conversations within leadership teams, especially leadership teams that are run by entrepreneurs. An entrepreneur probably sees some of these same issues I'm discussing in the book, and this will give the entrepreneur a way to talk about these problems with his or her team. I have shared many experiences in this book, and I believe these experiences can help start a conversation within your business that will solve some major roadblocks.

In life, most success comes from talent and discipline. In many cases, you can't increase your talent quickly. However, one thing you can increase very, very quickly is your discipline.

I named the book Wake-Up Call because when that alarm goes off, you have to decide what you're going to do. We've all had those experiences of getting those wake-up calls and going right back to sleep, but it's discipline that gets us out of bed and makes us take action on that wake-up call.

Maybe your wake-up call is that you're running out of money in the business, maybe you have more drama than normal, or maybe you have poor execution. When you get that wake-up call, are you going to apply the necessary amount of discipline to solve that issue? This book will amplify your wake-up call for your business. Will you apply the appropriate amount of discipline?

How can you use this book? Many teams have weekly meetings to talk about outstanding issues, so bring one chapter a week to discuss. Find a chapter that might be a wake-up call for your current situation, and use my experiences as a jumping off point to have that conversation.

———

Important Recognition: I have many coaches and mentors in my life that have influenced me, and it is important to recognize that many of the concepts and experiences in this book are formed by their input. I can't give everyone credit, but I want to just say thank you and recognize that many of these ideas were inherited from the people that helped me along the way.

My dad, Gordon Wyant, was my first technical mentor, and without the skills I learned from him I would have never been able to start my businesses or sell anything. He also taught me to be nice to hotel front desk attendants, and being nice helped us to get a better room.

Ken Vanderberg was my first business mentor, and he taught me the importance of patience. He also gave me some of my most frank feedback and challenged me to get a job after I failed at my first two startups. Ken has also been my longest-running mentor, and he has always been there when I needed him. Mentors come and go, but Ken has always been there since 1992. (I talked to him just last week).

Chuck Hegarty was the best business partner I ever had. He was also the best sales mentor in all of my 30 years of sales experience. I owe Chuck a lot for my success in business, and without his guidance, I might not be where I am now.

Bruce Gobdel was a mentor who came into my life at almost the same time that I experienced a perfect storm. We had a short stint as mentor and mentee, but he was critical to my successful exit in my last business. He brought reason to the insane world I was living in.

Will Ditzler was my first Scaling Up coach, and he was critical to our success with Scaling Up in my last business. While he wasn't a mentor, he was a great coach. He saw dysfunction and called it out. I have a great story I will tell someday about how he fired us as a client. (By the way, it was the right thing to do).

Bob Rabbit is a colleague who helped me as team member mentor. Bob speaks truth to power and has been a good friend.

Matt Reid, another colleague and team member mentor, has

always challenged me technically and professionally. I upped my game with Matt in my life.

Chris Booker has been a good friend and a friend/mentor for over 20 years. He's always been an encouragement in any new business endeavors. He has been a wise counsel — sometimes without him even knowing it.

Also, it is important that I recognize the authors and thought leaders that I have read over the years.

First, I need to recognize Verne Harnish, author of *Scaling Up*. He influenced the concepts in this book, the actual writing, including the structure of people, strategy, execution, and cash.

Here are a few of the books and authors that influenced my thinking:

Scaling Up: How a Few Companies Make It . . . and Why the Rest Don't by Verne Harnish

Good to Great: Why Some Companies Make the Leap . . . And Other's Don't by Jim Collins

Disney War by James B. Stewart

Let's Get Real or Let's Not Play: Transforming the Buyer/Seller Relationship by Mahan Khalsa

The 4 Disciplines of Execution: Achieving Your Wildly Important Goals by Chris McChesney

Shoe Dog: A Memoir by the Creator of Nike by Phil Knight

Topgrading: The Proven Hiring and Promoting Method That Turbocharges Company Performance by Bradford D. Smart

Multipliers: How the Best Leaders Make Everyone Smarter by Liz Wiseman

Predictable Revenue: Turn Your Business into a Sales Machine with the $100 Million Best Practices of Salesforce.com by Aaron Ross and Marylou Tyler

Blue Ocean Strategy: How to Create Uncontested Market Space and Make the Competition Irrelevant by W. Chan Kim and Renee A. Mauborgne

Trillion Dollar Coach: The Leadership Playbook of Silicon Valley's Bill Campbell by Eric Schmidt, Jonathan Rosenberg, and Alan Eagle

Humanocracy: Creating Organizations as Amazing as the People Inside Them by Gary Hamel and Michele Zanini

Turning the Flywheel: A Monograph to Accompany Good to Great by Jim Collins

What Got You Here Won't Get You There: How Successful People Become Even More Successful by Marshall Goldsmith

Nine Lies About Work: A Freethinking Leader's Guide to the Real World by Marcus Buckingham and Ashley Goodall

The Infinite Game by Simon Sinek

The Vision Driven Leader: 10 Questions to Focus Your Efforts, Energize Your Team, and Scale Your Business by Michael Hyatt

Profit First: Transform Your Business from a Cash-Eating Monster to a Money-Making Machine by Mike Michalowicz

Hyper Sales Growth: Street-Proven Systems & Processes. How to Grow Quickly & Profitably by Jack Daly

The Future Is Faster Than You Think: How Converging Technologies Are Transforming Business, Industries, and Our Lives by Peter H. Diamandis and Steven Kotler

Antifragile: Things That Gain from Disorder by Nassim Nicholas Taleb

PART I

PEOPLE

1

THE PERPLEXING CASE OF THE EMPLOYEE WHO QUITS ... BUT DOESN'T LEAVE

Every company strives to keep its employee retention rate high. You don't want to be spending excessive time interviewing, training, and bringing people along in new jobs. It saves time and money when you can keep the people you already have. So, if you haven't lost a lot of people, you're probably quite pleased with your retention rate.

However, is your retention rate as good as you think it is?

When an employee quits and leaves, that's disappointing, but at least the situation is clear. You know what you need to do. However, what about the employee who quits ... but doesn't leave?

I'm talking about the employee who is still physically present but has mentally checked out. I'm talking, of course, about the employee who shows up for the job every day but doesn't really *do* the job anymore.

You might describe these people as bunnies. The bunnies are very cute, but they are basically useless. They don't do much of anything — apart from hopping around and seeming pleasant. Many companies have employees like that.

These employees might maintain a very positive attitude toward the company and its mission. They may embrace the company's values. They may absolutely love their colleagues. They might even love the boss. However, they're not accomplishing anything, and you've got to do something about it.

This problem is unusually common in the fog of the 2020s, but it's nothing new. People become disconnected from their assigned responsibilities for all kinds of reasons. If you're paying attention as a corporate leader, you should notice it quickly. You must address the situation when an employee seems disconnected and fails to perform.

This is about accountability, but it doesn't have to be a harsh process. When someone has a decent attitude but isn't performing, that's not acceptable. However, it is often a problem you can solve. It starts with confronting the issue candidly and then trying to identify the disconnect.

If the person likes the company and wants the job, you need to find out why he or she is not *doing* the job. It might be something completely unrelated to business. It could be a problem at home that's making it hard for that person to focus. It could be that the employee no longer understands how his or her job fits into the company's larger picture.

Most of the time it's not that the person is lazy. Most people don't want to sit around and collect a paycheck for doing nothing, although you certainly find your share of people who think they're "working" by playing corporate politics and the like. But people don't want to just sponge. They enjoy doing something if they do it well and they know it's making a positive contribution.

So, when you find yourself dealing with a bunny — one of those people who has essentially quit but is still hanging around — you need to get that person to tell you honestly how he or she got to that point.

This is uncomfortable for a lot of bosses because it's never pleasant to hold people accountable. And make no mistake, that's what's going on here. You must confront the person about his or her lack of performance if you want to have any hope of retaining that employee.

I have all kinds of sympathy for people who feel lost or out-of-place in their jobs. However, people have to perform, and you have to begin the process of separating yourself from them if they don't. (I use the term "separate" instead of "fire" because I feel the term "fire" is old school.)

Having said that, a constructive approach could lead you to a positive outcome. The person who has a positive attitude, but poor performance, is easier to save than the high-performing person with a negative attitude (we call these people terrorists). The bunny, who still likes and believes in the company, is going to be a lot more receptive if you say, "Your performance needs to improve, and I'm happy to help you make it happen."

Sometimes this will lead the bunny to admit a hard truth: "I don't know what to do. I'm not good at this job any longer."

That would explain a lot about why the employee is not performing. The person is probably avoiding tasks because he or she can't perform those tasks well. Of course, that doesn't get the company anywhere. You need people producing.

So, you dig into how things got to this point. Was the employee poorly trained? Is his or her job description unclear or nonsensical? Is the person in the wrong seat on the bus, and in need of a reassignment?

It's always possible that a person isn't performing because the person's skills don't suit what you need. If that's the case, you need to assess how that person got hired in the first place, but in all likelihood, you're going to have to begin the process of separation. Hopefully, in most cases, you can work with the employee to redeem the situation. If that happens, you get an additional producer without having to spend any additional money.

Either way, the problem of the employee who quits but doesn't leave has to be resolved — one way or another. The presence of such a person is toxic for productivity as well as team chemistry, and it ultimately undermines your leadership if you let it persist. First, find a way to help that team member become productive. If that doesn't work, start the process of separating yourself from this employee. Everyone in your company needs to be productive, and you have to make sure that this happens — even if your bunny has to start hopping toward a new home.

Wake-Up Call: People decisions are the hardest decisions. Stop avoiding them.

2

THOSE TERRIFYING SITUATIONS WHEN YOU HAVE TO TELL A COLLEAGUE, "I DON'T TRUST YOU"

M ost people would recognize lack of trust as an issue in business. However, the mere lack of trust is not as deep as the problem can get.

How much of a problem is it when people don't trust each other, but they conduct themselves as if they do?

In today's business world, there is a lot of mistrust. There is also a lot of pretending. Admitting to a colleague that you don't trust him or her is an extremely uncomfortable proposition. Even admitting to yourself that you don't trust a colleague is difficult.

However, when we carry on as if nothing is wrong, we do a disservice to everyone involved.

Understanding the problem begins with recognizing where mistrust seeps in. Some years back, a colleague decided to share a story with me from his high school days. He went on at great length — and with lots of enthusiasm — about how every morning he would pretend to be going to school, only to sneak over to his girlfriend's house. After they would, er, *spend time together*, he would then move on to the things he was supposed to be doing.

He told the story with great pride, figuring I would enjoy hearing about how clever he was at his deceptions.

As I listened to this story, and noted the complete lack of any remorse at his dishonesty, I thought to myself, "Why should I trust this guy when he not only lied to his parents, but years later he's still apparently proud of it?"

I should have told him that his story had impacted my ability to trust him. However, I kept working alongside him for several years as if there was no issue.

That wasn't fair to him, to me, or to the company. As far as he knew, everything was fine, but the decisions I made concerning his role on the team were being influenced by my lack of trust in him. However, he had no idea that was the case. Neither did anyone else on the team.

Any chance of our business relationship reaching full fruition was destroyed, not only by his silly story, but also by my failure to express how it affected me.

I should have sat down with him and explained the situation. I didn't because I feared how it would go. "I don't trust you" is hardly something you want a colleague telling you. He probably would have had no idea why I felt that way.

If I had gotten it out in the open, there might have been a chance to resolve things. Maybe he could have told me something that would have allowed him to regain my trust. We'll never know because I never gave him the chance.

I have seen this same scenario play out many times in the companies I've coached. There is almost always someone who's telling a colleague, "I trust you," but who's walking around thinking, "No, I don't."

Obviously, this isn't the sort of thing you can just blurt out. You have to express it in the right manner. There are tools you can use that can help. One is Patrick Lencioni's book *The Five Dysfunctions of a Team*.[1] Another is Steven Covey's book, *The Speed of Trust*.[2] Both have tools that can help you approach a difficult conversation like this one.

A facilitator can help you have a difficult conversation, such as the one I just mentioned. A trained counselor or mediator is also a great resource, but it doesn't always have to be a paid professional. Sometimes it helps just to have a mature person who is respected, who can prevent the dialogue from getting too heated, and who can help the respective parties understand each other.

This will never be an easy conversation, but not having it will cause much more damage than fighting your way through it.

If there's one thing I want to make sure corporate leaders understand, it's this: There are people walking around your business right now who think, "I don't trust you" every time they pass a certain colleague.

Although they are thinking it, they're probably not saying it, and they're probably not giving the person they don't trust an opportunity to address the issue. Sometimes it's a simple matter of oversharing, like my former colleague with his high school story. Sometimes it's an action or a conversation the person won't even remember.

Without addressing it, that lack of trust will simmer under the surface, not announcing itself to anyone. Although this lack of trust is seething and seemingly hidden away, it undermines the goals of the company and the relationships among its team members on a daily basis.

Although you don't want to say, "I don't trust you," the refusal to address the situation is undermining you every day. Enlist a mature and respected person to help you broach the subject.

Wake-Up Call: The work environment is one of the few places we are paid to fake trust.

3

MOST PARTNERSHIPS DIE, AND MOST PARTNERS DON'T SEE IT COMING

I t's easy to feel good about the idea of a business partnership. Two friends, two acquaintances, or two professional associates who share a vision . . . starting a business and conquering the world together.

Then one day, way in the future, they'll be able to tell the story of their partnership and how they couldn't have done all they did if they hadn't done it together.

It's too bad almost none of them end up that way, but it's not that surprising either. Most partnerships aren't built to last, because businesses change, and people change. Sometimes one of the most unproductive things you can do is try to preserve a 50-50 partnership in a business that's evolving away from it.

I'm not opposed to partnerships per se. I have simply observed over time that almost all of them end up dead at some point. If you're thinking about becoming part of a partnership, maybe what I have to say here will help you prepare for some eventualities that have happened to many others in your position.

If you decide not to become part of a partnership because of this chapter, that's fine, too. My point here is not to persuade you one way or the other. It's just to make sure you're aware of what has happened to many who have gone before you.

One of the most fundamental weaknesses of partnerships is that they tend to be set up by attorneys. Now I have nothing against legal professionals. They play their role very well. However, when an attorney sets up a partnership, he or she deals with the *logical* aspect of the contract. An attorney invariably misses the *psychological* aspects, and those are usually the seeds of the partnership's demise.

Legal constructs don't run partnerships. Entrepreneurs do. And while entrepreneurs can be great visionaries and hard workers — and without a doubt, high achievers — they can also be naïve about some things.

One of those things is the reality that the partnership is probably going to end at some point. I realize no one wants to come right out and say that when they're just getting started. You want to express all the confidence in the world that you're in it for the long haul. Maybe you feel like it would be a betrayal to include exit protocols in your partnership agreement, but it's a huge mistake not to because things change.

For example, it's common in the early days of a partnership for the partners to take modest salaries to keep costs low. I once consulted with a company whose partners did that at first, but soon one of the partners became a parent. He felt he needed to draw a higher salary to support his wife and baby. The other partner was single, and he saw no need to take a raise. However, they had to make the same money because they were 50-50. The two partners disagreed over salaries, and it became a point of conflict.

Neither was right or wrong. They were just in different positions, and they had different priorities. The partner whose wife had a baby wasn't wrong to become a father. The other partner wasn't wrong to remain single. It was just who they were, but it made the partnership structure harder to sustain. (They didn't make it past three years, by the way.)

Partners who don't talk through the complexities of the partnership — including different scenarios that could affect the business and their roles together — are setting themselves up for a difficult dissolution down the road.

However, even if you do have that discussion, there are some things a legal agreement can't prepare you for: Humans get offended. They have egos. They want things, and they change over time. What made all the sense in the world to you at 30 makes no sense at all when you're 45. What you once were sure of, doesn't seem so certain at a different point in time.

Once you were willing to work 24/7 to build the business. Now you want a vacation. However, your partner might not care about taking a vacation, and you're concerned you'll seem like the lesser contributor if you go on one.

Once you were ready to work until you had both feet in the grave. Now you're starting to think retirement doesn't sound so bad, but you didn't structure the partnership to account for that. So, what do you do?

To make matters worse, it's not only people who change. Businesses change, too. Often, the basic structure and value proposition you started with give way to different directions as you learn things — positive and negative — from your experiences.

Let's say you were originally going to sell auto parts to local retailers, and one of the partners had great connections with all the retailers, so that partner got the job of selling. However, you soon realized the industry doesn't work the way you thought, and there were better strategies for distributing your product. So, you had to make an adjustment. Nothing wrong with that. It happens all the time. However, the sales partner didn't have connections with people in the new distribution channels, so suddenly his role isn't what either of you expected. The new role probably doesn't justify 50 percent of the profits.

However, he's 50 percent owner, so what do you do now? The two partners are no longer as complementary as they once were, and it's not so easy to retrofit them into the new realities.

Finally, there is this uncomfortable reality: Partnerships that start with friendship can't necessarily be sustained over the long-term with that same friendship, because friendships evolve based on experiences.

Your best friends in college might not still be your closest friends once you're married and raising kids. As you get older, you move to different stages of life, and you share different kinds of experiences with other people. If you become business partners with a friend, your friendship isn't going to be the same in two years, because you've both been through different things. It might be better. It might be worse, but it won't be the same.

Keeping a strong relationship with your partner is something you both need to work on frequently. The partnership will only work if both are willing to put in the necessary effort.

Basically, a business run by partners requires the constant maintenance of two things — the business and an interpersonal relationship. A business run by just one owner requires just the maintenance of the business.

That doesn't mean partnerships can never work. Obviously, some do go the distance. However, yours is far less likely to do so if you don't understand these issues up front. And if your partnership does come to an end at some point, that just means it's like most of the others.

When forming a partnership, think about all the complexities before writing a contract with an attorney. How will you handle changes in the business? What will you do if one partner wants to retire? What type of exit protocols do you need? Enlist your attorney's help with the details in the contract only after you have agreed and thought through each stage.

Wake-Up Call: All partnerships eventually end, but most don't end well. (If you think your partnership is just okay, you're probably in more trouble than you think.)

4
___

ARISTOTLE'S THREE KINDS OF FRIENDS, AND HOW THEY IMPACT YOUR BUSINESS

___

F riendships in the workplace are a big challenge, but you don't find many business books or articles about the subject — partially because we don't have good definitions about what friendships mean or how they impact life at work. I like the simplistic view Aristotle used for friendship, and I believe it applies to the workplace.

Aristotle had insight into the business world long before it took any modern form. In today's world — and in Aristotle's world — much of business revolves around relationships.

Before we talk about the business application of these relationships, let's dive into Aristotle's different types of friends. The way he saw things, there were three different kinds of friends — the utility friend, the pleasure friend, and the friend of good.[1] Although Aristotle used the term pleasure friend, I'll call these people "fun friends."

The utility friend is your friend because you are useful to each other. That doesn't mean you don't like or care about each other. What it does mean is that the primary basis for the friendship is mutual interest.

This person might be your friend because you work together, or you are in the same running club, or you volunteer together. You have good work chemistry. Your skills complement each other's. This is a good friend to have. However, you can't forget that the basis for the relationship is a mutual interest. Take that away and the friendship probably doesn't survive.

The fun friend is a straightforward concept. You're thinking of going to some sort of festival, and you don't want to go by yourself. Who can you call? Jim! Why? Because he's a riot. You'll never fail to have a blast when you're in Jim's company.

There is nothing wrong with a fun friend. There is nothing wrong with having a good time with other people. However, you have to recognize that when you're not engaged in some sort of exciting activity, you might not have that much to discuss with Jim.

Then there's the friend of good. This is the friend who will be there through thick or thin. The one who knows your virtues and flaws. The one who has been on hand for every struggle and every triumph, and will be sure to stick around, no matter what. Friends like these are more valuable than anything, and when you make one, you need to be sure to hang on to him or her.

The application for business is this: We're most likely, in the business environment, to make the first two kinds of friends — utility friends and fun friends. Obviously, you will make a lot of utility friends at work, because work is all about getting things done and finding people who can help you. Often, the utility friend you make at work becomes a fun friend as well. You work so well together that you figure you might as well make lunch outings a regular thing or get together after work. Now your life is even more tied up with that utility/fun friend.

When you spend a lot of time with a person as a utility and fun friend, you tend to want that friend to become a friend of good. You feel like you know each other well. You get along great. Why not expect your utility/fun friend to become the type of friend who will be there for you no matter what?

Utility and fun friendships can not only break down, but they can also cause issues in the workplace. The reason is simple, but the implications are complex. The friendship that's based on utility can survive as long as the utility factors are in place. The friendship that's based on fun can survive as long as you two are having a blast.

However, in both cases the friendship is conditional. It depends on the aforementioned factors remaining viable and serving as the underpinnings of the relationships. Take those factors away, and there's still a chance the friendship could thrive. Sometimes people do grow genuinely close, but there's also a good chance that the friendship will fall apart from lack of the common bonds that held it together.

The most important lesson here is to know what kinds of friends you have, and not to make the mistake of misjudging these relationships. Utility friends and fun friends are great. However, especially in the work setting, keep them straight and attune your expectations accordingly.

By all means, seek all the friends of good you can get. They're tremendous, and yes, I've made some in business. However, know the difference between a real friend of good and a utility friend, and avoid depending on a friend of utility.

I can tell you firsthand how fast utility friends and friends of fun can disappear when business relationships end. When I exited my last business, it was sudden and unplanned. While I had many friends in that business, almost all of those friendships ended when I left the business. (I can count on one hand the number of friends I still have from those business relationships.) I don't blame anyone for that because that's just the way most utility friendships end.

Why is that important? As an entrepreneur, when you are building your business, you're going to make a lot of friends. Just know that those friends are friends of utility. When you're the owner, boss, or founder, you often have more utility friends than you know what to do with. That's great being friends with those people, but just know those people are friends of utility. When that business relationship ends, it's very likely that the friendship will end too.

. . .

Wake-Up Call: Friends you make at work are usually utility/fun friends. Don't expect your utility/fun friends to act like real friends.

5
———

HIRING FRIENDS: WHY AN APPEALING
IDEA ALMOST NEVER WORKS

———

W hen I launched my first business, I hired a lot of friends. I'm
not sure I could have gotten the business going if I hadn't.

A business that's just launching will have some trouble attracting
employees, because no one is sure of the company's staying power or
financial strength. Your friends are more likely to work for you
because they know you, and they feel comfortable with your style of
business management. That's why a lot of startup CEOs will
surround themselves with friends. In the beginning it feels both
necessary and comfortable, not to mention the fact that it can be fun
working with people you already know and like.

The problem comes down the road. For the vast majority of
companies that employ friends of the CEO, the arrangement only
works for the first year or two. After that, someone – if not everyone –
inevitably ends up disappointed.

When you hire people you don't know, you can enforce levels of
performance. The situation is vastly different with one of your
friends because you know all that person's flaws. This makes it harder
for you to focus solely on performance.

The arrangement presents challenges for the CEO, as well, when the business starts to grow. More people will join the company, and the CEO will have to manage the whole team using policies and principles that apply equally to everyone. However, the employees who joined the company, after the initial wave of friends, are soon going to recognize that a certain group hangs out socially with the CEO. In some cases, there may be an effort to include the new people, but when you join a bunch of people who've been friends for years, you're not on the same level with them. You're going to recognize that.

Close friendships can become an issue when you have to make decisions that involve managing people and holding them accountable for their performance. When it was just you and some of your friends in the early days of the company, you could probably get away with a pretty loose approach to management. You all knew each other. You all had personal relationships. You could deal with each other on that level.

Now that the company has grown, you have new employees you can't deal with in that way. How do you handle that? Do you have one group you manage with professional policies and procedures, while you deal with the other group – your old friends – in a light and informal manner?

To avoid favoritism, do you make everyone follow professional policies and procedures? If you do that, how will your old friends feel about the fact that the company doesn't have the warm, informal feeling it did at the start?

This is why hiring friends almost never works over the long term. All this seems so obvious, yet business owners do it all the time. Why? Because people can always convince themselves they will be the exceptions to the rule, and that's not a completely bad thing. We wouldn't have any pioneers or trailblazers if people didn't believe that.

If you are convinced you're the rare exception who can make it work, I'm not telling you not to hire friends. However, I would plead with you to think through the issues I've outlined here, and possibly talk with your friends about them before they come on board. At least that way, when things change over the course of time, they won't be able to say you didn't warn them.

Working with friends is a very appealing idea. That's why so many people try it. As I said earlier in this chapter, I tried it and I had some success, but in the end, I was disappointed, and my friends were disappointed. So, know what you are getting into.

Wake-Up Call: Hiring friends can create problems at work — for both you and your friends. Think through the issues ahead of time and have a candid conversation with your friends before you hire them.

6
_____

HOW TO CREATE THE FIRST TEAM
WITHOUT MANAGERS

_____

The book, *Humanocracy,* is a game changer, and it expands on "The End of Bureaucracy," an article from Harvard Business Review's November-December 2018 edition.[1] This article excited many people in the business world because it highlighted Haier, an appliance business, that removed middle management. (You can just imagine the cost savings of that!)

After reading the article, people could see the benefit of removing middle management, but they didn't understand the details on how to do it. *Humanocracy* explains the details missing in the Harvard article.[2]

Humanocracy is a new model of management that tries to eliminate as much bureaucracy as possible. Although the book is based on very simple concepts, the concepts are hard to implement, and this can make it a difficult book to read. The implementation of the strategies it suggests will be challenging. It's like saying, "I'm going to lose weight by summer." We all say it, and we all want to look better in our swimsuits, but very few people actually do it. It's easy to say that you want to lose weight, but you have to eat better and move more. It's a simple formula. It's the same way with the book *Humanocracy*. The book is long, and it has a lot of data and research in it, but the concepts are very simple.

There were two chapters in this book that made a huge impact on me — Chapter 10 and Chapter 12. Chapter 10 discusses the power of community, which is so vital for a humanocracy. For a long time in my career, I shied away from community. I wanted to be able to do things on my own, and I wanted to be able to take credit for my achievements. I thought in a bureaucratic mindset: If I do it on my own and I'm the smartest person in the room, then I'll be promoted and excel. So, I didn't promote community.

What I learned 5-10 years ago was that I was missing so much opportunity by not promoting community. I, as a person, could excel and grow faster in community than I could trying to be a sole operator.

I first learned the value of community by mistake and out of desperation, and it led to one of my best growth opportunities of the last twenty years. In 2010, my company was working with a large software company that was also competing with us to deliver consulting services. That competition was not only negatively affecting my company, but it was also making it nearly impossible for me to stay in business.

Out of desperation, I created a coalition of my competitors who also worked with this software company. As a coalition, we identified our mutual challenges, and we put pressure on our mutual partner, the software company. At the time, we would have been happy if the software company would have just made changes in its practices, but because we made a coalition, we were able to get the company out of the consulting business.

This created an enormous vacuum of unmet need that I, along with the other partners, was able to rush into. In this case, not only did community make us better, but it also made us a lot more money. The craziest part is that it was a community of competitors — organizations that would not typically build community.

The other crucial chapter is Chapter 12, "The Power of Experimentation."[3] This is something that Jim Collins also wrote about in *Great by Choice.*[4] The greatest companies shoot bullets, not cannonballs. They shoot bullets so that they can calibrate their strategies. Once they have their strategy calibrated, then they will shoot the big cannonball.

In *Humanocracy*, the authors expand on this concept about experimentation. One of my biggest pet peeves with entrepreneurs is their desire to constantly experiment. To make matters worse, they like to experiment with the big things.

Please learn from others' mistakes. Don't experiment with the big things. I know some entrepreneurs who like to make huge changes, but do everything possible to avoid that.

Once you've created the good habit of shooting bullets, not cannonballs, please limit the constant firing of bullets in your business. Even though Jim Collins gives you this analogy of firing bullets, he also encourages you to establish your flywheel and to turn it over and over and over. (He wrote extensively about this concept in *Turning the Flywheel,*[5] and I've also written about it in the chapter "Whatever You Do, Don't Abandon Your Flywheel.")

I have seen far too many entrepreneurs ruin a perfectly good flywheel with too much experimentation. They basically shoot it full of bullets.

Please go read the book *Humanocracy*; it's part of your dedication to becoming a life-long learner. Then experiment with the ideas in it before making a big change and removing management. It's possible to reduce management and have every member of the team actively involved in decision making. However, don't get so excited about experimentation that you forget to focus on your flywheel.

Wake-Up Call: Playing Superman — or trying to do everything yourself — and avoiding community are two things that are costing you personally.

7

WHEN PROMOTING FROM WITHIN GOES WRONG

N o CEO is ever going to get an argument from employees when he or she announces, "Our policy, whenever possible, is to promote from within."

On the surface, this seems like a good approach. Your existing employees know your culture, your systems, and your corporate goals. They won't need a lot of onboarding. The organization won't have to get used to them.

The fact that your employee sought a promotion suggests at least some level of loyalty to the company. Plus, if your employees know you'll promote from within, that provides an incentive for them to do well and try to earn those opportunities.

No wonder none of them will argue with this policy, but maybe some of them should.

Hiring from within is usually the popular thing to do, which tends to make it the easy thing to do. It's certainly the path of least resistance, unless you promote a very unpopular employee. However, sometimes promoting from within is a gigantic, missed opportunity, and sometimes it's an abject disaster.

Let's start with the missed opportunity scenario. Companies who want to grow and improve simply have to open themselves up to fresh ideas and different perspectives, and the best way to do that is to bring people in from the outside, who have been different places than you have been. They're familiar with practices and ideas you're not — not because they're necessarily better than you, but simply because every company's perspective is limited somewhat to its own experiences.

Perhaps your company needs to hire a new chief operations officer, and you've got employees already on the team who meet the minimum requirements. They've had good reviews, and they're well liked. Why not give one of them a shot?

However, let's say there's an operations professional available who has learned effective manufacturing practices that your team isn't familiar with. Given the chance, this person would shore up weaknesses and introduce new efficiencies to the factory floor.

You think you're doing reasonably well now, but this person would come in and see opportunities to make changes and take things to a new level. It would mean a dramatic boost to both your productivity and your profitability.

How do you know such a person exists? Well, that's my point. If you always promote from within, you don't, and it's because you're not even going to look. That internal hire might make some changes and some improvements, but given his or her company pedigree, the internal hire is likely to keep the broader systems more or less what they've always been.

That might be fine. However, if you missed out on an opportunity to do way better than fine, what could that cost you down the road? How much harder might it be to grow and achieve stretch goals when you didn't even look for the person who could have gotten you there?

Then there's the abject disaster scenario, and I witnessed this firsthand early in my career. At that time, I got a job in IT with a local hospital. I was a rare hire, in that I was from the outside, and I was asked to provide leadership to an IT team whose challenges were significant. Almost everyone else on the team had been hired from the existing internal team, because this hospital had a strong philosophy of hiring from within whenever possible.

It was a train wreck. Some of these people had been nurse's aides or patient financial counselors. They weren't IT professionals, but they had some computer proficiency, and the hospital decided that was good enough to put them in the IT department under the "promote internally whenever possible" philosophy.

It was the worst IT department I have ever worked with, and it was hard to blame the people. They should never have been put together as an IT team in the first place. The hospital's management did that.

There was no way you could lead them into better performance, because they simply lacked the talent. There's a big difference between someone who knows his way around the computer, and someone who really understands information technology. Almost no one on this team did, and the hospital paid a huge price because its systems needed a serious upgrade — and there simply wasn't the talent to get it done.

The "promote from within" philosophy didn't just make the IT department bad, it made the whole hospital bad. To this day, my family has strict instructions. If I get hurt or fall ill in that city, medevac me to another city. The hospital is that bad. If you're wondering which hospital this is, I'll never tell.

Now having said all this, I am not against promoting from within in all cases. However, I think companies need to be smarter about when it makes sense to do it and when it doesn't.

It makes far more sense if you're promoting within your core competency. If you've earned a reputation as an excellent furniture manufacturer, then it makes perfect sense to promote people who have proven themselves within your area of core competency. These people are the ones who made your company the best, so they should get the opportunities to go further.

However, every company also has to do well in areas outside their core competencies. The furniture manufacturer also needs a good CFO, a solid IT director and an excellent janitor. When you're hiring for those positions, there's no reason to be stuck on promoting from within. Search everywhere you can for the best financial, IT, and maintenance professionals, and hire the best person you can find.

Then let those outside hires support the internal professionals who continue to excel at your company's area of core competency.

I understand the inclination of corporate leaders to reward their own people first. This tends to happen when companies hover around the 50-employee mark. It feels like a family, and you want to take care of the family members above all else. I get it.

However, sometimes the best way to take care of the family members is to bring in talent from outside that can strengthen the overall performance of the organization. Sometimes it's not so helpful to put one of them in a position that doesn't fit.

Hire from within when it augments where you're already strong. But everywhere else? Cast a wide net and see what kind of talent you can bring in to make your team even better. That's truly a strategy that rewards everyone.

Wake-Up Call: Do not make assumptions on the best way to hire or promote. Evaluate what makes the most sense for the position.

8

RULES FOR STAYCATION

R ecently, I took a week off, but I didn't go anywhere. My goal was to stay home, sleep, read, relax, and recharge. The vacation didn't start as a staycation, but the combination of some cancelations, and some reading I have been doing on recharging, convinced me to just stay home.

I'm a strong believer in the need to recharge. I strongly encourage my team at Red Wagon to take a vacation. In my previous job, I would even go as far as making it a point to review people's vacation schedules during yearly planning meetings.

If I think someone doesn't have enough vacation built in, I ask them to consider some four-day weekends or another week in the summer. Our team requires rested and refreshed minds to tackle the complex work we do, and so does yours. This thinking goes back to what Covey talked about in his book, *The Seven Habits of Highly Effective People*.[1] You can cut more wood in the same amount of time if you take a break to sharpen your saw. The same is true when it comes to vacation.

As part of my recent staycation, relaxing and recharging were critical. My wife and I sat down to plan. We cleared the calendars, put off projects, and planned days of total inactivity. I have to tell you, for the most part, it worked. While we made it work, it wasn't easy. The challenge is that life just gets in the way when you are at home. We found ourselves returning to the same routines of our normal life. It was a constant battle to relax and recharge. Basically, it was a battle to do nothing, which is extremely hard for me.

This leads me to advice for anyone planning to recharge at home — don't. When you are away from home, you can't run to that dentist appointment, and you can't take the kids to basketball practice. You are forced to vacation. You can focus on doing nothing.

If, like me, you find yourself forced into a staycation, here are some best practices:

- Cancel all appointments. Don't take the kids to any appointments or practices; they wouldn't go if you were in Florida.
- Put down the tools. It is so easy to tackle that to-do list around the house. Don't do it! For most people that won't recharge anything.
- Order-In. I try to always eat healthy, especially when I'm home. It's the easiest place to eat healthy, but it is work. Try to cut down on the work. Nothing says you aren't on vacation like cooking. Do your best to order in, but order in healthy food.
- Don't see friends. It seems like a good idea to have friends over, but maintaining friendships can be one of the most draining things. A true vacation is when we all get a needed break from our friends.
- Don't run errands. Nothing eats into relaxing time and kills a recharge like driving around in traffic, fighting crowds, and trying to shop.
- Plan your time. Sit down and plan what you are not going to do. Today, we are not going to do laundry.
- Turn off Wi-Fi and cell service for a day or two, minimum.

You will be amazed at how refreshed you will feel. These bright objects drain a significant amount of energy from us, even when we are using them for fun!

- Go outside! Staycations can be cold (if you live in the north), but if the sun is out, get out. The vitamin D you get on a real vacation is a huge value to the recharge. You still need to get some; get out there and soak it up! Make the time to truly recharge; you need it!

Wake-Up Call: If you don't take a break, you will break. Instead, make it a practice to have mandatory vacations.

9

HUMANS: PSYCHOLOGICAL BEINGS IN A (SORT OF) LOGICAL WORLD

R emember Mr. Spock on *Star Trek*? You probably remember the pointy ears, but the main thing Spock was known for was his logic. As the story went, Vulcans were completely devoid of emotion, so everything they said and did was solely based on logic. Sometimes Spock could be cold and clinical, but he was on the side of good, and you always knew his actions were 100 percent driven by logic.

What made Spock such an interesting character is that we know people like that don't exist. It's not so much that we're emotional — although that's part of it – but we are far more psychological beings than we are logical ones.

That doesn't mean we're lacking in intelligence. It just means that human patterns of thought are driven by more than cold, hard data. They're also driven by attitudes, impulses, and patterns that are shaped by our experiences, or perhaps simply by the unique chemical wiring that makes up the 3-pound brain in everyone's head.

This is hardly a new observation, but I wonder if the prevalence of our devices today has caused us to lose sight of it.

Just about everyone these days carries around a device that fits in his or her pocket, which is the source of almost unlimited logic. That is, if you can find a reliable source! The nature of technology is to spit out information that is driven by objective fact. The financial statement either balances or it doesn't. It either rained or it didn't. The Lions either lost or . . . well, they probably lost.

Having access to such logical devices may be giving us an unrealistic expectation of logic in people. It may also cause us to think that any factor in a person's reasoning apart from logic deserves to be rejected.

That is not only untrue, but it also completely misunderstands human nature. Mr. Spock would surely dismiss it as completely illogical.

Because we are psychological beings — influenced by our experiences and our chemical makeups — we often find it's impossible to get two people to see things the same way. Some examples are simple: You're terrified of spiders, but I don't mind them at all. You think department meetings are a waste of time, but I think they're helpful.

These aren't objective matters of fact, but that doesn't mean there's no value to the various perspectives. This is how it works with humans because there is more to people than cold, hard logic. On some matters we have opinions, and those opinions influence the way we understand and apply the objective facts.

The question is how we account for this in business. We don't want to quash people's individuality that's based on their psychological makeup. However, we do need certain behaviors based on fact.

Think about it like this: If you were about to get on a flight, what would you think if you were told the pilot had two checklists to choose from? One is the standard Boeing checklist, and the other is Captain Bob's preferred checklist.

With all due respect to Captain Bob's opinions and preferences, you'd probably feel better knowing that he didn't blow off the Boeing checklist.

People in business need to be able to accept that certain things require standard procedures, built on data-based fact. There is plenty of room in business for opinions, attitudes and even feelings. The trick is for management to know when to make room for those things, and when there is no wiggle room to vary from procedure.

Knowing all this, it's important to understand human psychology if we're going to solve problems. Diplomats are trained at this. It's how they get to resolutions for all kinds of situations between people who are predisposed not to agree. If you have someone in your company with those kinds of skills, they're worth their weight in gold. Put them to good use.

But recognize that, no matter what you do, logic is only *part* of the human makeup. Don't lament that. Choose to accept and understand the psychological side of humans. The other parts are good, and they're part of who we are. However, we must learn to recognize when we must rely totally on solid data to make decisions and when we can allow emotions and opinions to enter into the equation.

Wake-Up Call: Humans are psychological, not logical. Don't treat them like logical beings.

10

WHAT I LEARNED ABOUT FAMILY AND
BUSINESS ON THE FOURTH OF JULY

———

I didn't get to go to a Fourth of July parade with my family in 2020, because there wasn't one. It was the first time since 2001 that I did not join my family for a parade on the Fourth.

There's a reason I've maintained such a streak, and it's because I learned something in July 2001.

If you can think back that far, you'll remember that the country seemed to be flying high. We were three months away from 9/11. The economy was going gangbusters. The tech bubble had burst, but we hadn't felt the full effects yet. My business was also going gangbusters at the time. I felt like I had found my niche, and that the team I was part of was getting ready to make a serious impact on the business world.

So, I was excited when I got an invitation to spend the Fourth of July hanging out with some guys from work. We weren't doing any business. We were just having fun, and it seemed like a great opportunity to bond with these people. After all, we'd be sharing great business adventures together.

The two kids we had at the time (we've since added two more) were very small and very cute. In spite of my decision to spend my day elsewhere, my wife decided to go ahead and take them to the parade.

In 2001, digital cameras were not yet the norm, so the photos she took at the parade still had to go through the usual process of 24-hour film development. She took them in right after the parade, and I went with her the following day to pick them up.

It was then that I realized the mistake I had made. As we opened up that yellow envelope full of photos and thumbed through them, I saw my kids experiencing the excitement of that parade. I realized I had missed my chance to not only see it as it happened, but to experience it with them. These photos were wonderful, but all they represented to me was a missed opportunity.

I asked myself: If I'd declined that invitation to hang out with the guys from work, would I ever have seriously regretted it? No, I wouldn't have. But would I regret missing that parade with my wife and my two small children? I certainly would, and I still do.

That opportunity was lost, but I could at least make sure no others would be. I made a decision right then and there to never miss a Fourth of July parade with my family again, and I never have. From 2002 through 2019, we made every single one together. Eighteen in a row. If the parade had happened in 2020, it would have been 19.

I often hear people talk about matters like this by asking the following question: What do you want to be remembered for when you die? What they're getting at is the question of your legacy, and whether you'd want to be remembered for business accomplishments or for being loving and taking good care of your family. I get it. But honestly, that's not what motivates me.

Making these parades is not about what people remember about me when I'm dead. Who cares? I'll be dead. People's good or bad memories of me won't make any difference to me at that point.

No, this is about my own experiences in life. It's about realizing what I lose if I miss these moments. It's about being able to sit around and tell stories of what happened at the parade. I don't want to just hear about the parade because I decided hanging out with the work guys was more important.

Sure, I understand there's some value to bonding with work colleagues. There are times when it makes sense to invest your time in doing that. However, I can't emphasize this enough: Don't do it at the expense of those special moments with your family.

If you ever find yourself in a situation in which your spouse is getting ready to take the kids to something you could and should also be going to – and it's because you chose something work-related – think long and hard about that decision.

Whatever career benefit you think you're going to get from missing the family event, is it worth what you'll be giving up? When you thumb through the photos with your spouse later on, and he or she laments that you weren't there, will you feel confident then that you made the right call?

Your work buddies will be fine without you. You will have other opportunities to get together with them. Those special moments with your kids come and go, and they don't come back.

Wake-Up Call: Don't think about what people will say when you are dead. Instead, think about how you will feel today. Make the right call.

PART II
—————
STRATEGY

11

THE ONE-PAGE PLAN: ESCAPING THE HAZE, AND FINDING THE WHY

The other day I was sitting on my back porch looking at the summer haze, and it occurred to me: This summer haze that I am seeing is just like the haze people sometimes experience in business.

Some people simply lose their sense of what they are supposed to be focused on and why they should be focusing on it. Once that happens, they're in trouble. However, there's a way to get it back, and it's not complicated. Verne Harnish, the founder of the Young Entre-preneurs Organization, now EO, is a big advocate of one-page plans. They can be used in a lot of ways. You could have a single one-page plan for your entire company, or you could draw up one-page plans for specific initiatives of the company.

However, a great way to use the one-page plan is to have one for every single day. You might wonder if this isn't just a fancy version of the to-do list, or of the Franklin Planner. However, a one-page plan for the day can have a lot of elements to it — what needs to be done, the resources that will be required, and the time it will take. You can customize it to what works for you. The most critical thing the daily one-page plan should include is the why, which is key. It's also hard.

Ask yourself: Why are you adding that extra product line? Why are you going to put this employee under disciplinary action? Why are you going with a new vendor? Why are you swapping out a certain piece of equipment?

If you don't identify why you're doing these things, you may be performing tasks without considering how those tasks fit into the company's priorities and overall objectives. That can lead to mistakes, because you can get so zoomed in on the task, you might pursue the task in a way that doesn't advance the bigger goals.

Identifying the why to every task helps to solve that problem. It keeps you out of the haze. It keeps you focused not only on the things you need to do, but also on the role each of them plays in getting you where you are trying to go.

By clearing up that question, you help to keep yourself laser focused. You're in a better position to get it done — and done right. Also, I think that is especially important now with so many people easing their way back into what used to be normal to them.

I have done hundreds of these one-page plans. These plans don't have to take you hours. Once you've got the one-page plans down to a science, it shouldn't take you long to start each day getting one ready. These plans keep you focused. They keep you productive and they keep you effective.

They keep you out of the haze. It's one thing when the summer heat and humidity make you feel like you can't see where you're going. It's another thing when you've having that problem running your business.

Don't let the haze of everyday tasks take you away from the bigger picture. Keep focused on your priorities, objectives, and annual goals, which are often listed on an annual one-page strategic plan.

Like coffee, the one-page daily plan and the one-page annual strategic plan help clear the mental haze. The daily plan helps you focus on your most important items of the day and helps you to consider why each of these tasks is important. When thinking about why each task is important, consider how the task fits into the company's priorities by taking a look at the one-page annual strategic plan. When you compare the two plans, you'll be able to do work that matters and brings you closer to meeting your company's goals.

If you want more information about planning and Scaling Up, visit my website at <u>www.redwagonadvisors.com</u>

Wake-Up Call: Don't let the daily haze block your view of annual priorities.

12

THE RISK-AVERSE ENTREPRENEUR'S LAMENT: I REALLY SHOULD HAVE GONE FOR IT!

H ere's a myth about entrepreneurs. I bet you've heard it: Entrepreneurs aren't afraid of risk! Are you sure about that?

There are a lot of reasons people start their own businesses. They believe in an idea they have. They can't stand having a boss. They love the idea of unlimited earning potential.

I'm not sure love of risk is high on that list. Sure, you take a certain risk by going off on your own, but even that's overstated. Your business could fail, and you could be without income. However, when working for someone else, you could get fired tomorrow. There's some risk to anything you do.

The truth is, to hit it big, entrepreneurs could use a bit more tolerance for risk than I think they sometimes have. I include myself in that category. It's something I've had to learn over the years.

Aversion to risk won't necessarily stop an entrepreneur from starting a business, but in too many critical cases, it stops the entrepreneur from going all out on an opportunity that could have meant everything to his or her enterprise.

In the right situation — when the facts are clear and the metrics look good — the right move is to defy all fear and go for it. It's always better to go all out than to go halfway. Yet, too often, entrepreneurs don't go all out because they're nervous about the risk.

I'll give you two examples from my own history to illustrate the point. About 15 years ago, when I was early in my entrepreneurial journey, I had an opportunity to take my business in a different direction. I did lots of research, and the metrics looked excellent. It would have required me to part ways with some people I was working with at the time, and they weren't too thrilled about it. However, the facts told me it made sense to jump on the opportunity, and I decided to do it.

However, in the course of the next 24 hours, fear set in. My situation at the time didn't hold the promise of this new one, but it was reasonably stable. I had a family with young children. The risk started to worry me, and then fear set in.

I reversed course, didn't take the opportunity, and stayed on the path I was already on. I gave in to fear. Looking back now, I've watched how the situation that presented itself developed, and I realize I would have had significant success with it. The fear I gave in to was unfounded.

The issue was mostly security, but there was a little ego involved, as well. Had I taken the opportunity, I would have endured a short-term step backward in my perceived prestige. It would have been like leaving the corporate executive suite and working in your basement, and that wouldn't have looked like a step forward.

None of these are reasons to pass up a solid opportunity. I feared the risks that were involved, so I bailed.

I regret it, of course, but it's one of those experiences you learn from. Another thing I've learned is that half-measures are worse than no measures at all.

The second time I let fear change my mind was about eight years ago. A very hot piece of technology created another opportunity for me. Many of my clients were interested in it, and they wanted to see me invest in the technology so I could put it to work on their behalf.

There was some other technology I was already using for many of the same purposes, and it was making us money. However, it didn't have the promise of this new innovation. Indeed, the new one could do things that would have taken my clients to new heights — and us with them.

Despite the advantages of the new technology, I was hesitant. To be clear, I was hesitant to completely abandon existing technology that was making us money. It made me nervous, but the best course of action was to burn the ships and go forward with this new technology. It would have given them better results very quickly.

To add to my own nervousness, my partners did not want to take this radical course. Instead, they talked me out of moving forward in a bold way. So, I split the difference. I brought in the new technology but also kept the old. I was hedging my bets. I should have burned the ships. The approach I took confused people. Was the new technology better? If so, why not give everyone the full advantage of it? Why keep the old if it wasn't as good?

Worse, I kept finding things not to like about the new technology. Finding flaws was my way of defending my decision not to fully commit to it. I developed a bias born of my fear. I was looking for something to confirm my fear and doubt, and I grabbed onto anything that seemed to fill that need.

Some of my team felt better with the cautious approach, and I was sensitive to their concerns. However, that proved to be a failure on my part as a leader. All the facts said the new technology would perform for us and for our clients, and my job as leader was to show the team that without dismissing their concerns.

Instead, I let uncertainty and doubt creep in, and that doubt built upon itself, as it so often tends to do. The benefit I could have gotten from fully committing myself to this opportunity eluded me.

Understand, I am not talking about wild risks. Neither of these scenarios fits that description. In both cases, I had done my research, run the numbers and double-checked my findings. The opportunities were solid. I was just nervous, and the risk bothered me too much in both cases to pursue these opportunities as I should have.

Fearless entrepreneurs? I wish it was true. However, as we go along, we can all learn that risk is nothing to be afraid of.

The requisite risk and reward analysis is always necessary, of course, but when the facts clearly tell you to move decisively, will you?

Or, will you let fear hold you back? I let fear hold me back in these two instances. I've learned. I hope you will learn from my mistakes instead of having to learn from your own.

Wake Up Call: Most of us take far too little risk. After doing your due diligence, don't be afraid of taking risks and moving forward with great opportunities.

13

THREE PATHS TO GROWTH: WHICH ONE FITS YOUR COMPANY?

E very business owner wants to achieve growth, and every business owner should. So, it makes sense that, when you're seeking growth, you should be able to answer a basic question: What is your primary path to growth?

Everyone's answer to this question will include some basic fundamentals, such as focusing on great products and services and focusing on taking care of customers.

However, beyond those fundamentals, there are three primary paths to growth that apply to all industries. I often find that corporate leaders aren't entirely sure which of the three best suits their companies. As a result, they're going full-bore in all three directions, and often wearing out their people in the process.

Here are the three:

Organic growth. This one is the most basic. The company growing organically is not trying to change the world with its products and services, but it's finding small innovative moves that can differentiate it from competitors.

Innovation, combined with a world-class sales and marketing

effort, keeps the orders coming in and the revenue expanding. This play can grow faster with better strategy and/or patented, defensible intellectual property, or IP.

Execution plus acquisition. Have you perfected the execution of your product or service well beyond the industry norm? Are your systems and processes far more efficient than those of your competitors? Great. Ride that excellence to happy customers and strong cash flow. Then you can grow by acquiring your competitors at a value price and increase their value by implementing your systems and processes to replace their old, inferior ones. I made that sound *much* simpler than it is, but if you can achieve that level of excellence, this is definitely a great path to growth. This is sometimes called a roll-up play.

The Unicorn. All the world loves big ideas, and some of the most successful companies in history have been built on them. If you operate in the business world, it's only natural to believe you're capable of coming up with the next innovation that will change everything — the next unicorn. This is a strategy with high potential, but it also has high risks and very long odds. So, if your entire growth strategy is based on coming up with a unicorn, you'd better find it. Any good unicorn needs to be defended. So, you will most likely need something exclusive — something that may require a patent — to protect your unicorn.

Now you know the landscape. The entrepreneur has two main problems when pursuing growth. First, many of them pursue growth that is not aligned with their real strengths or opportunities. Second, they pursue all three without a real commitment to the one that makes the most sense.

What is your best path to growth? To answer that question, you must look at the strengths and opportunities of your company. In addition, you must consider your market positioning and the capabilities of your people and your processes.

Ask yourself: Do you execute the basic fundamentals extremely well, and sell your products and services with exceptional success? Then your primary path to growth might be organic.

Is your execution so strong that you're running circles around your competition? Then maybe you should consider bringing them into your organization and consolidating your hold on the market.

This is not to say you shouldn't try to excel at all aspects of your operation. Does it make sense to seek organic growth while also striving for excellence in execution? Of course, it does. You want to do everything as well as you can. However, you're trying to grow *right now*, and the focus of your growth strategy should be on the path your company can pursue most successfully based on its structure and positioning today.

But what about the unicorn? What about the big idea that could change everything? Why shouldn't you pursue that? Didn't Steve Jobs? Didn't Bill Gates?

Of course, they did. And so have a lot of other people whose names you've never heard of, because they didn't become Steve Jobs or Bill Gates. I love big ideas, and I am the last person who's ever going to tell you not to pursue one.

However, here's what you need to know: Big ideas usually take a long time to come to fruition. It never feels that way when they first come to you. You get inspired and you start imagining all the places your idea can take you.

You might even call your team together and share your vision, and they might get very inspired, too. Once they've heard your idea, they'll head back to work feeling inspired to make it all happen.

This can be trouble. That idea is probably a very long way from realization, if it ever happens. Your team is excited now, but in six months they're going to wonder if this is ever going anywhere. If all you do is focus on the unicorn, or the big idea, then you may not experience much growth.

You can have your big idea, and you can chase after it. Yet in the meantime, your path to growth has to be based on where your company is strongest and most capable right now. Your team needs to be focused on that.

There's nothing wrong with having select, strategic people helping you push toward an exciting innovation, but how are you going to make it happen if you're not growing and earning revenue from your existing operations? Your team should be focused on growth and revenue to fund those innovations.

Which of the three paths to growth fits your company best? It shouldn't be a hard question to answer if you know your company and your people. Once you've decided on which path fits your company, list at least five things you can do to pursue growth on that path. For example, if you chose organic growth, what are five things your company can do to grow organically? Keep your company focused on pursuing that path and implementing those steps that lead to growth.

Once you have chosen your path and have your focus on five steps to pursue growth, the most important thing you can do is stay committed to that path. I have mentored and coached far too many entrepreneurs who play a game of whiplash with their companies, constantly changing the strategy for growth and never getting it. Take it from me; I'm also speaking from personal experience.

Wake-Up Call: You can have it all. You just can't have it all right now. Pick one path to grow and to get it all . . . eventually.

14

MY GUILTY PLEASURE

I'm going to admit it. My guilty pleasure is McDonald's. I'm embarrassed to tell you about it, but there are a couple of possible culprits, or reasons why McDonald's might be such a guilty pleasure for me. Growing up, my family and I traveled on the weekends. My dad was a traveling pastor, a missionary. When we got out of a late-night service, we would stop by McDonald's on the way home. We would split a French fry, and we would get a couple of hamburgers. We would all split that, and that's what we had for dinner on the way home. I really enjoyed that, and the taste and smell of McDonald's brings me back to a simple and happy time with my family.

Growing up in Generation X in the 1980s, McDonald's was a staple. However, when I lived in remote parts of Canada or Brazil, there wasn't a McDonald's nearby, so I would go years without McDonald's. I was so excited to get it when I came back to the States.

Unfortunately, as an adult and by my own choice, I deepened that addiction. It's still with me today, so I know almost everything there is to know about McDonald's. I've even watched the documentary about the McDonald's Monopoly fraud, *McMillions*.[1] It's one of the best case studies about internal fraud out there. If you watch that HBO series and you're not convinced you should have more audits on your business finances, then you didn't watch the same documentary that I did.

I love McDonald's. Over the years, I've skipped around the menu. I've been a Big Mac guy and a Quarter Pounder guy. When I have been trying to diet at McDonald's – I know you can't diet at McDonald's — but when I've been trying to reduce my caloric intake, I've tried to eat chicken nuggets, salads, or wraps.

I remember as a kid it was always impressive when we went to McDonald's and the sign told me how many hamburgers they had served. During the '80s and '90s, they were counting up the hamburgers sold. Then the sign changed, and it said that billions of customers were served.

McDonald's had already realized that all that mattered was how many burgers or customers were served. They counted and measured that and were very open with those numbers. McDonald's knew its hedgehog. The company knew this before Jim Collins popularized the idea of a hedgehog or a flywheel.

What is your hedgehog? In *Great by Choice*, Jim Collins asks three questions to help you find out:

1. "What are you passionate about?
2. What can you be the best in the world at?
3. What drives your economic engine?"[2]

McDonald's still knows its hedgehog. They serve hamburgers consistently and quickly to a lot of people. McDonald's took that hedgehog, built it into a flywheel, and spun it over and over again. They have focused on principles that Jim Collins suggests, and they practiced them even before he wrote about them. McDonald's knows what its company is best at. When you look at McDonald's, you'll see an amazing application of a hedgehog and a flywheel that Jim Collins talks about in his books *Good to Great* and *Great by Choice*.[3]

What is the payoff for this article? Look at what McDonald's did during COVID. The company returned its focus to its hedgehog.

McDonald's has lived through many recessions in the past decades, but none of them was quite like COVID. They had to focus on their hedgehog to make it through the pandemic.

Jim Collins writes about the hedgehog in his book, *Good to Great*.[4] When you find your hedgehog, it's the one thing you'll go back to over and over again. It's what businesses turn to when they're under stress, when they get into challenges, and when they get into trouble. Successful businesses will always go back to their hedgehogs.

If you have the same guilty pleasure that I do — McDonald's — you'll notice the same thing that I did. Of course, they had to shut down their dining during the initial stages of the COVID pandemic. However, they had to change one main thing to save them during this time. If you're a connoisseur like me, it's obvious the one thing that changed. It was the menu. These huge beautiful electronic displays went from wraps, salads, cinnamon rolls, and chicken tenders to a few hamburgers and chicken nuggets.

Go read *Good to Great*. If you understand Jim Collins's principles, you'll understand that this is what McDonald's has done. They went back to their hedgehog when they got into trouble — when everything shut down during the pandemic.

The bottom line is that you've got to focus on your hedgehog. You've got to be doing what you're passionate about, what you are the best in the world at — or could be the best in the world at — and what drives your economic engine. Do it now, because in the next recession your business could depend on it for survival.

Wake-Up Call: If you don't have a defined hedgehog and flywheel, you will fail . . . eventually.

15

WORK ON YOUR BUSINESS, NOT IN IT

———

Have you ever been to a soccer game where the players were 5 and 6 years old? If so, you might have noticed some similarities to many businesses. In fact, you might have noticed a pattern that could explain why your business isn't growing.

At the start of the game, all the players are set in their positions just where the coaches told them to play. How well they understand their assignments may be another matter, but at least they know where to stand.

Then the ball is kicked off. At this point, all focus on positions and assignments is lost, and every single one of those small children manically runs after the ball. It's the funniest thing to watch, and we've all seen it. It's a pack of 10 little kids following the ball around until a goal is scored or a timeout is called. Then everything resets, and the exact same thing happens again.

Now you may say, they're 5 and 6 years old. I know, and that's a pretty decent excuse for them. However, how do we explain the same behavior from many companies, especially the companies' leaders?

Many corporate leaders approach their businesses in a way that is remarkably similar to that group of 5-and-6-year-old soccer players. They know their roles, and they know what they're supposed to be doing every day, but they can't stay disciplined enough to stay in that rhythm and get it done.

In other words, they can't stay in the mode of working *on* their businesses because they keep getting sucked into working *in* their businesses.

This is not my original concept, of course, and much of my thinking here was influenced by the book *The E-Myth*,[1] along with its follow-up, *The E-Myth Revisited*.[2] You will recognize the phenomenon I'm talking about when you read these books. The leader should be thinking, strategizing, building bridges, and communicating a vision. In other words, the leader should be leading.

However, once the day starts, the leader gets sucked into every little thing going on within the business. An issue arises with a customer, and the CEO is right there. An attractive RFP, or request for proposal, arrives, and the CEO dives in. A scheduling challenge comes up, and the CEO is front and center addressing it. What is worse is that many of the other team members jump in around the CEO, like that pack of kids around the soccer ball.

It can be so many things. Continually stopping your work and answering emails. Jumping in to address a supply issue. You knew you were supposed to focus on leadership-type issues, but dang it, the day just got away from you. Just like the next day will.

The problem isn't limited to just CEOs. Much of upper management can fall into the same trap. How many problems have arisen within your company that result in the CFO, the CIO and the HR director all being *right there* to handle the situation?

How many brains does it really take to solve these problems? Aren't there already people who are being paid to do this? Don't you have confidence in those people? Then let them do it. Corporate leaders can't keep their hands off this because they're addicted to execution. It's understandable on a certain level. Good business leaders love what their companies do, and they love being part of it. Yes, there's some leadership benefit to remaining close to the company's day-to-day functions. Employees do respect a leader who isn't afraid to get his or her hands dirty to help get the job done. However, more than that, employees respect a leader who leads.

Someone has to provide the vision and the direction, and if you're too busy doing what you're paying *them* to do, who is going to provide that vision and direction?

Your employees do appreciate help on the little things, but not as much as they appreciate your strong and solid leadership.

I face this challenge, too. This morning, I was trying to finish up an offering we call Red Wagon in a Box, which is a set of tools any business can use to help achieve growth, and the emails kept coming. I had to keep telling myself: *The emails can wait. Finish Red Wagon in a Box.*

Why do I face this struggle? Because I like execution, too, but my job is to lead. When the leader is able to focus on leading, the benefits are compelling and tangible. They start with growth.

When leaders are setting things up to position the company for growth, it allows all that hard work the rest of the team is doing to pay off. The leader has to be able to figure that out.

Another benefit to focusing on leadership is a high-functioning culture. You'll avoid things like system breakdowns, missed deadlines and botched assignments. The leader must design processes that enable the business to run smoothly and efficiently, and the leader must empower other leaders to work that system effectively every day.

It's counterintuitive for some leaders, because they think the way to achieve a high-functioning environment is to keep their hands on everything all the time. It's not. It's for them to provide solid leadership and allow their team to work the plan.

Can you do this? There's always some emergency you could jump on. There's always some work you could insist on reviewing. There's always some reason you could run down the hall to the printer with your hair on fire. However, you're not working on your business when you are doing the work you hired your team to do.

Even 5-and-6-year-olds know the object of the game is to score, and you'll score more often when you play the game of business as a team. Stop chasing after the ball all the time and let each team member play his or her role. Your job is to lead the team, not to play every position. So, focus on designing the processes and enabling your team to implement them. Work *on* your business, not *in* it.

Wake-Up Call: Let your team play their positions. Don't play their positions for them.

16

CREATE AN ANNUAL CALENDAR

A n annual business calendar can make a tremendous difference in your business. However, many small to midsized companies make excuses for not having a calendar. I hear the excuses all the time. Some businesses tell me, "It's not important at this stage of the business." While others say, "We are too small, and we don't have time."

I understand that sometimes a business is too small for certain things. If you have ten employees, you probably are too small for an HR manager, but you are not too small for a calendar!

Even if you just have one employee, you should still build an annual calendar. It allows you to plan better for the year, and it helps you clarify what will be happening. Sometimes our plans for the year are not feasible.

Bill Gates said, "Most people overestimate what they can do in one year and underestimate what they can do in 10 years."[1]

Human propensity for overestimating what you can do in a year is exasperated when you don't have a company calendar. It's akin to not counting the money in your bank account and just spending it. Time — like cash — must be carefully spent.

When you don't look at a calendar, you run out of time and don't realize where it's been. Make an annual calendar for your business every year without fail. However, if you haven't built a calendar yet, just go ahead and do it. There's still a huge value in creating one.

Calendars help show you when you will be busy and when you will have slowdowns; they also help you predict the future. Calendars can help you determine problems with productivity that might occur when July 4th occurs during the middle of the work week. You might not have as much productivity during that week as you do during a typical week.

Calendars bring a level of clarity into business. Often entrepreneurs, business owners, and founders rely on running a lot of the business in their heads. They have almost crystal-clear clarity of what their businesses look like going into the future.

However, as soon as you hire employees, those employees have a lot of questions. What does the vacation schedule look like? When are the holidays? When do we get paid? When do we do strategic planning?

Building a company calendar is partially for you, but mostly it's for the people you work with — your staff, your partner companies, and your customers.

Put all your holidays and company meetings on the calendar, including your quarterly meetings and celebrations. Don't forget to include future conferences, birthdays, and work anniversaries. I'd also encourage you to add deadlines for customers to make sure they get met.

When you have finished your company calendar, sit back and take a look at it as a whole. A calendar is like a mosaic; you can't see the impact of a year from looking at a day or a week. As you zoom out from the days, to the months, to the year, what do you discover? What needs to change? What constraints do you see?

Don't worry about having a perfect calendar before you publish it. You can always update it. Some people don't publish a calendar because they spend too much time trying to perfect it.

You might be wondering, "What's the best format to use?" There are many electronic calendars you can use. I always recommend the calendar that is the easiest one for everyone to use and maintain. That might be the calendar on Microsoft, Google, or another platform.

Calendars help business owners plan better, see the future with more clarity, and discover constraints and changes that need to be made. Do you have one?

Wake-Up Call: No plan is complete without a calendar.

17

DON'T HIRE A SALESPERSON (AT LEAST NOT IN THE INITIAL STAGES OF YOUR BUSINESS)

————

I understand why you find the idea of hiring a salesperson for your brand-new company appealing. You want to grow, and to grow, you need to sell. If only you could bring on a crack sales professional who would go out, book the meetings, impress the prospects, and close the deals for you.

You'd gladly pay commissions, and maybe even a salary, for the growth a great sales professional would bring you. Best of all, you wouldn't have to make the sales yourself!

This is why, as an entrepreneur fervently seeking growth, you want so badly to hire a salesperson. I get it. Resist. I implore you. In the early stages of a company, you are not ready for a salesperson yet.

This is advice I have given to so many entrepreneurs, and most don't listen to me. I hope for your sake you'll be one of the rare ones who does. This is one of the most critical — and most common — mistakes entrepreneurs make. By hiring a salesperson, they think they're going to solve all kinds of problems. In all likelihood, you will *not* solve problems by hiring a salesperson, but you will introduce a whole bunch of new ones into your organization.

First of all, most entrepreneurial organizations don't have an established sales process in place. They think that's what they're hiring the salesperson to do, and the salesperson probably claims to be able to implement such a process.

There's a difference between doing the selling and designing the sales process, and most effective salespeople can't create the process.

So, a full-time salesperson comes into a fledgling organization that has no established sales process. To make matters worse, the company probably lacks many of the tools a salesperson would need to be successful. The salesperson also lacks institutional knowledge of the company. This means the entrepreneurial CEO is now spending even more time on sales than before — teaching and training the new sales whiz.

Finally, there's a disturbing fact most CEOs don't know about salespeople. While some will hit the ground running, most require a year to get up to speed and start delivering any sort of return on investment. So, the entrepreneur who was hoping the salesperson would improve margins ends up making the margins worse. Why? Because the entrepreneur has to pay the salesperson, and for months on end that person doesn't sell anything.

You are transferring your wealth to another person the moment you hire that salesperson. Up until now, you were bringing tremendous value to your company because you could not only run it, but you could also sell it at no additional cost. Now you're taking on an additional cost, and if the salesperson is not successful, you will never get back the wealth you gave away.

It's also been my experience that good salespeople are change agents. They're always looking for ways to change every organization they touch. Now you might think, good! That's what your customers are looking for! However, guess which organization will be the first they want to change? Yours. If they come in and find your company isn't mature enough to support what they envision themselves doing, they're going to sow dissension.

There's a better way to do this. By the way, I'm not against *ever* hiring a salesperson. There is a time to hire someone, but the time is not when the founder/entrepreneur/CEO is getting tired of doing it and is getting antsy for the growth to pick up. The time to do it is when you've matured as an organization to the point where a salesperson can step into a mature, prosperous environment and help take it to the next level. Taking the right path to get there is the key.

It starts with hiring, not a salesperson, but a sales navigator. Now what does the sales navigator do? Simply, the sales navigator shares the burden of doing the sales with you. Yes, Entrepreneur, you're still going to do the sales. However, there's a lot about the sales process that the sales navigator could help you with, which would make it less time-consuming and more efficient.

Not only that, but the sales navigator can work with you to create that formalized sales process you don't have now. The sales navigator can help you work through mistakes you make in the process. You need to correct these problems before you're paying a high-level salesperson to be frustrated by those same mistakes.

Right now, with you doing the sales, the whole process is likely in your head. You may know it, but there's no way you could teach it to another person because it's intuitive to you. Working with the sales navigator will force you to let the process become more regimented.

This is still an investment, but it's a much smaller one — maybe 20-to-25 percent of what you would have invested in a salesperson. And because the navigator will immediately strengthen your existing sales efforts, rather than starting at ground zero and having to ramp up, you're likely to see results much sooner.

You'll also learn a great deal about how the sales process works. A lot of that comes from when the sales navigator asks, "What do I do next?" When you're not sure of the answer, the two of you will have to figure it out together. That's the best kind of learning.

And when you and your sales navigator have accomplished so much that you're twice as busy as when you first considered hiring a salesperson, that's when it's time to take another look at it. Your processes are mapped out, and your value proposition is clear and easy for you to teach. You're not desperate for new revenue. Rather, you're prepared to invest some of your healthy revenue stream into strengthening the solid sales process you've already created.

Final thought: You won't find the term sales navigator posted anywhere because it's a made-up term. If you decide to look for a sales navigator, look for someone with some sales experience and the ability to learn. You can find someone who is short on experience, but long on talent. Hire this person to be your first sales navigator.

Wake-Up Call: Hiring a salesperson won't solve your sales problems. (Building a better sales process will.)

18

CUT-RATE FACILITIES USUALLY ANNOUNCE THE PRESENCE OF A CUT-RATE ENTREPRENEUR

———

The condition of a facility is something that I notice as soon as I enter the building. Many times, the entrepreneur I am calling on has a beautiful, well-maintained facility. Other times, I run into a building that is hopelessly antiquated or hasn't been updated in years. Or, it doesn't look like there was an architect involved or consulted when it was first designed. (You should've seen my old building. In my defense, I didn't have a choice.) Maybe the entrepreneur's building has been updated, but clearly the update was on the cheap end of things.

Then you sit down with the founder of the company, who starts telling you about the building. He's very proud of it. He did most of it himself, and to this day he's the guy who figures out how to make it work when deficiencies show themselves.

I hope this doesn't offend you if what I'm saying sounds familiar, but a cut-rate building usually signals a cut-rate entrepreneur.

This is not to judge any company's humble beginning. I know we all have to start out with whatever facility we can handle. Some start in their own basements or garages. Some start in the spare corner office of a friend's company. Often, your first facility is all you can afford, so you have to make the best of it. However, this is as much about mindset as it is about the building itself.

As you grow, a solid entrepreneur understands the importance of investing in better digs, and in people who can help to make the surroundings better.

It isn't necessarily money that's the issue here. It's more about the mindset that says, no matter what the challenge is, "I can figure this out myself."

Maybe you could, but if there's someone who can do it better than you can, why wouldn't you get people like that to help you? You'd get better results, and you'd elevate your whole operation. This is a limitation too many entrepreneurs put on themselves.

When I meet an entrepreneur who seems to exhibit these traits, I ask, "Would you be willing to make a fundamental change in the way you operate your business? Would you be willing to sell this building and upgrade? Would you be able to invest in a real update that would transform your company?"

I'm talking about moves that would exhibit maturity and professionalism. If the entrepreneur is unwilling, believing he can just keep fixing the building himself, that tells me something.

I don't give up on companies like this, of course, but this sort of thing shows me these entrepreneurs are likely to remain stuck at their current level.

Often, I find that these kinds of entrepreneurs got where they are by relying on uber traits that helped make them successful. They've got great vision and real drive. They're excellent at articulating the why of their companies. These are the personal traits they trust in themselves.

What they often don't see is the limits of these personal traits to elevate important aspects of the business. They're surrounded by an unprofessional business environment that was clearly done on the cheap. Instead of coming up with ways to make it better, they'll tell you all day long about the deals they got on what they have.

This is not to say there's no wisdom in finding ways to control costs, but you might compare it to a difference between buying a slightly used car to save a little money . . . and driving a beater.

A friend of mine recently bought a 2019 Lexus. It's a very nice car, even if it's not brand new. He figures he saved $10,000 or more by picking a car that's slightly used and has close to 15,000 miles on it. That's good, and no client is going to question him if he picks them up for lunch in a 2019 Lexus.

However, let's say he picks up the client in a 1987 Pontiac Grand Prix. It's got bald tires and tape holding the mirrors together. If you're the client who gets picked up in that thing, you don't want to be judgmental, but you're wondering: "Just how effective a businessman can this guy be?" You're communicating to the client that you'd rather hang on to a dilapidated Grand Prix than find a way to upgrade.

Maybe you're comfortable in your old clunker. Maybe you've even installed a sound system that's worth more than the car, and you're jamming as you drive. To you, this is great.

Yet, what it says to everyone else is that you're falling short in maturity and professionalism. You're making the same statement with the outdated building that needs to be transformed or replaced.

With many entrepreneurs like this, it's as much a mental block as a fear of spending the money. Trying to make that rundown facility work is what they're comfortable doing. Yet, they're sending a signal to the rest of the business world that they'd rather keep operating in that space than let someone else take them to another level.

By all means, start your business wherever you can. But if you don't show a willingness to let go and grow with something as fundamental as your facility, you're announcing to the rest of the business world that you're willing to accept those limits on yourself and on your business.

Their expectations of you are probably going to track pretty closely with the message you're sending them, and if it's that message, it will not help you succeed.

. . .

Wake-Up Call: Be aware of the perception that's created by your business environment.

19

SALES IN TOUGH TIMES: GET THE RIGHT PEOPLE SELLING THE RIGHT THINGS IN THE BEST WAY

There's probably never a time when selling a product or a service is easy. However, before COVID, booming economic times made it possible for a lot of people to have sales success without elite skills.

Maybe your company has had sales success in recent years. Maybe some of your salespeople have had success, even though it's more due to the strong economy than their own skills. That might lead you to think you can ride through the tough times that have now arrived with the same team. You can't.

While we all hope to get through this as quickly as possible, there's no denying the economy has hit a major rough patch. When the situation is different, you have to think differently about a lot of things. You have to tighten up some things you would normally treat with a looser attitude.

Sales is at the top of that list. In times like this, you must have the right people selling the right things in the right way, or best way. There is no room for variance from that standard, especially now. So, what does that mean?

Let's start with the right people. There is no mystery attached to identifying your best salespeople. Performance metrics cannot be faked in sales. If you pay attention to your team, you know who's proactive, who's tenacious, who's effective, who's attentive to details, and who knows how to close.

The numbers tell that story, but you can also see it in the way your people operate. The people who fit that description need to be on your team. These are the people who know how to rise above a difficult environment and still show clients the value of continuing to buy. The salespeople who were just riding the wave for the past several years are not going to make it.

That brings us to the right things. What you're selling is just as important as who's selling it, and this is no time for experimentation. You know the products and services that represent your business's core strength — that best represent your value proposition. Those are the ones you need your sales team focused on.

Salespeople can get distracted — and get you distracted — by ancillary things. They can get all kinds of ideas about clever approaches and unconventional strategies. They can get it in their heads that the key to success is to focus on something other than your core strength. Don't let them.

When times are tough, you have to focus on your strength. It's hard enough to stray from that even in good times, although that's when you can get away with it because you've got a margin for error. You don't have a margin for error now. Make sure your salespeople are selling the right things — the proven performers that satisfy your customers and make you money.

Finally, make sure they're taking the best approach. I realize that begs the question: What exactly is the best approach? In his book *Hyper Sales Growth*, Jack Daly asserts that there is only one best, or right, way to sell.[1]

However, he doesn't define what it is because there is no definition. Every company is different. What Daly says, though, is that every company should be able to look at its own top sales performers and establish that the way they're doing it is the way everyone should do it.[2]

But wait, you might say, people are individuals, and some have different approaches to things. I'm sure they do, but if their approach isn't generating the results of the top performers, then their approach isn't the right one for your company.

There's a temptation at a time like this to throw your hands up and say to your sales team, "Just go find a way to sell!" They deserve better than that, and so does your company. At a time like this, process isn't optional. Process becomes more important than ever. This is when your salespeople need clear direction on how to sell, and this is the time when you need to be locking it down and making sure they're taking the right approach.

A good sales approach, after all, can be duplicated. If it's the way that works, a skilled salesperson can learn how to do it. As much as this might offend some salespeople, sales is not an art form. There's a right way and a wrong way to do it, and the right way is the one that's been proven to work within your organization.

Tell your people how to sell based on that experience. If they protest that this approach isn't a fit for them, then thank them for their time and wish them well with their next opportunity. You've got to get it right consistently.

One way to do that is to perform sales skills assessments. It can be a little tricky to do a skills assessment for someone who's been working with you awhile, and you might get some resistance.

Yet this is essential information you've got to have, so you'll know for sure that you've got the right people, selling the right things in the right way.

If this means your sales team gets a little smaller and a little more tunnel-visioned, that is not a bad thing. If it means their approach becomes more uniform, that's a great thing as long as it's the approach with a track record of working.

Sales is hard during a turbulent economy, and that's why it has to be done right. This is no time to experiment or to take chances with people who haven't done enough to earn your confidence. Get the right people. Make sure they're selling the right things. And insist they sell in the right way. Do that, and you've got as good a chance as anyone of thriving in the tough environment.

Much of the thinking in this chapter has been influenced by Jack Daly and his book Hyper Sales Growth.

Wake-Up Call: As Jack Daly says, there is only one right way of selling your product or service.

20

THE STRATEGIC PLANNING LETDOWN, AND HOW TO AVOID IT

————

Have you ever felt a letdown after Christmas? You know you shouldn't feel that way because you have all these nice new things, right? Then you realize that what's most special about Christmas is the experience — the anticipation, the sharing, the revealing, and the time with family.

At some point, with all that behind you, you kick back and look at all your new stuff. You feel a little deflated because Christmas itself was the best part and now it's over. I think this is a pretty close approximation of what many companies experience, and it's called Strategic Planning Letdown.

If you do strategic planning on a regular basis (and you certainly should), then you know it can be a fun, exciting and even inspiring experience. You go off-site, maybe for a day or two. You do some fun team-building exercises, and you set big goals that you expect to pay off in the form of a realized vision for the company's future.

By the time this strategic planning session is over, you might feel a little exhausted, but it's a great form of exhaustion because you can't wait to get to actually implement those goals and strategies.

Then you get back to the office. You've got 1,000 emails in your inbox. A supplier didn't come through with a shipment you needed. A customer is unhappy about something, and it has to be dealt with right away.

Sure, you want to do all the things you talked about in strategic planning, but today you need to take care of all this. Maybe tomorrow. Actually, tomorrow looks crazy, too. Maybe the next day. Or maybe not . . .

Before long, just about everyone who took part in the strategic planning session feels like the session itself was the high point. There's little to no follow-up. Why? It's because no one feels they have the time, or because there's no plan to put the ideas into action. Or, maybe it's because no one is taking charge to make sure it happens. It could even be some combination of these things, but as the disappointment of the strategic planning outcome sets in, people can become disillusioned.

Coming up with a big and inspiring new plan is great, but if the company doesn't show it can follow through, then the result could be worse than if you'd never done it in the first place. Now people will question whether it's worth their time to participate in future planning sessions since the track record suggests the company will put the giant pads of paper containing all the ideas in a closet somewhere — and never act on them. This is all very unnecessary.

When I take companies through strategic planning sessions, one crucial step is to make sure there are clear action steps to follow the session. We identify who is in charge of moving them forward. We assign action steps with timelines.

We even make sure these assignments are incorporated into the company's regular planning system, which will work whether the system is sophisticated like Trello or as basic as a typed-up to-do list.

I have a friend who owns a company consisting of two full-time employees. They share their to-do lists on a Google Drive document. For a company like this, following up on strategic planning priorities would get a big push forward by simply putting those items on the Google doc and making sure they don't get taken off.

With my clients, we always have a follow-up session 90 days after the initial one. So, there's a built-in incentive to move the priorities forward. No one wants to show up at the follow-up session and say they didn't do any of the things they agreed to do at the first one. Certainly, the CEO doesn't want to show up at the follow-up session and have everyone say the CEO dropped the ball because that's an indictment of the CEO's leadership.

The key to all this is to make sure the strategic planning session is more than just an uplifting, emotional, and visionary experience. It's fine for it to be all of that, but it also needs to be the start of an ongoing action initiative with real measurements of success.

Coming out of the planning session, if you can see how you'll undertake the action steps and achieve the goals, you've done a good job. If you've thought through the hurdles and you know how you'll tackle them, you're in a great position to get the most out of these efforts. If you return to the office with a different perspective on what you need to do and how you'll spend your days, then all this has been an excellent investment of time and money.

However, think all this through before you wrap up the session. Otherwise, the letdown is a real possibility, and you'll wonder why you ever did it in the first place.

Wake-Up Call: Don't get caught up in the emotional excitement of strategy. Leave room to execute your vision.

21

WHAT TO DO
WITH EMPLOYEES WHO ARE TAKING
THE SLOW WALK INTO RETIREMENT

———

Y ou've probably had one or two in your company. Maybe you've even worked alongside one or two of them. You know how to recognize them.

At one time, they may have had a vision. They may have been willing to take risks. They may have been interested in exercising leadership, but now they're running out the clock on their careers. They've achieved a certain position, and the only thing they want at this point is to make sure nothing disrupts them.

They're taking the slow walk into retirement. If you're not careful, you could let them take your entire organization down with them. This is a phenomenon among Baby Boomers, but to be fair to the Baby Boomers, that's just because many of them are in this position at the moment. It will probably be the same for Millennials in 20 years.

Maybe it's someone who's just moving into his or her 50s. We'll say it's a guy named Gary. Gary has a lot more of his career behind him than ahead of him. He's got a pension fund built up. He's 12 to 15 years away from drawing on the pension and collecting Social Security. He's got some savings. He's looking forward to walking away from work and enjoying it all.

Since that's not happening today or tomorrow, Gary can't afford to walk away from the job yet. What he refuses to do, however, is take any risks or rock the boat in any way. He has no ambition for promotions or anything like that. A raise would be nice, but he mostly just wants to protect his position and ride it out until he can walk away with all his benefits intact.

He's like the football team that's leading by three touchdowns with five minutes left in the game. They're not trying to score more points as much as they're trying to run out the clock. That's understandable in football because the game ends at the same time for all the players.

Yet that's not the case at Gary's company. There are younger employees who will be there 20 years after he leaves. For them, the game isn't ending. They need the company pursuing big goals, taking risks, and breaking new ground. Gary isn't interested in any of that. At best, he's not going to help. At worst, he's going to passively sabotage risky initiatives because he doesn't want his comfortable status quo being jeopardized.

This is especially difficult at companies where ownership is looking at a generational handoff. The younger generation may be eager to assume the mantle of leadership, but they are not going to be happy to inherit Gary, and Gary could even be in ownership, which makes the situation more complex. He's likely to be the biggest resister of the new generation's vision for the company, because it almost certainly means change for him.

So, how do you deal with someone like Gary in your organization? Remember, he's not only creating a problem by dragging his feet, he's also creating potential resentment and division within the company. You don't want your team dynamic disrupted by one retirement-slow-walker with a lackadaisical attitude.

This is where key performance indicators and operating performance reports make a big difference. If you can sit Gary down and show him data that indicates his performance is lagging, you've got a basis for a discussion with him about how to change it.

Companies that lack these measurements are just winging it with respect to assessing people's performance, and a slow walker like Gary can go hog-wild in a place like that.

It requires a very candid conversation and possibly a difficult decision. Gary needs to understand that the company has ambitious goals, and that it doesn't matter how long any particular team member plans to be there. Everyone must be fully engaged in the pursuit of the goals. You need some sort of follow-up and accountability — which Gary knows will be in place — to ensure he's fully engaged from now until the day he hangs it up.

Going back to our football team: Imagine a team makes the playoffs, and one of its offensive linemen is planning to retire at the end of the season. How would the quarterback like it if the defensive pass rushers were in his face all day long because that one lineman didn't want to risk injury in what could be the final game of his career? That's essentially what Gary's doing to his colleagues, most of whom have a very real stake in the long-term success of the organization.

While every leader prefers not to issue threats, Gary needs to understand that no job is guaranteed to anyone in the absence of performance. If he needs those 12 to 15 years to get across the retirement threshold, then he'd better start acting like the company's success is his priority.

By the way, I can tell you this for sure: No matter how old I get, the slow walk to retirement is not for me. I can't imagine becoming that risk-averse and safe and abandoning the pursuit of big ideas and ambitious goals. I've always been that way, and I'm confident I always will be.

Maybe the best way to deal with the Garys of the world is to pay attention when they're young and looking for a job with your company. Do they seem team-oriented and goal-oriented, and do they embrace your company's vision? Do they seem determined to do their part to see that vision realized, with the implied understanding that the company's success will reward them as well?

If that's the way they are when they're young, they're much less likely to turn into a Gary when they're in their 50s. Prevention is the best cure.

Wake-Up Call: Your company is too small to not have every employee fully engaged.

22

VERTICALS: YOU WANT TO GROW? START LIMITING YOURSELF

———

H as anyone ever suggested to you that you could grow more efficiently by limiting yourself? It sounds counterintuitive, but I'm going to suggest it to you now.

The instinct of many entrepreneurs is that limits are the enemy of growth — that you want to go everywhere and do everything for everyone. Accepting limits on any of this, the thinking goes, is the enemy of growth.

I want to challenge that thinking, and I'll do it by asking you to think in terms of verticals. A vertical is simply an area of focus, and just about all entrepreneurs would agree that some degree of focus is crucial. After all, you wouldn't create a company that makes soda pop, office chairs, vitamins, picture frames and saxophones. No one could possibly be good at all of those things. You need to do what you know, and that requires some level of focus for everyone.

So, we already agree that you can't do everything, and we already agree that some limits are helpful because they keep you focused on what you do well. That's what the concept of verticals is all about. I'm going to suggest to you now that you'll grow more — and more sustainably — if you embrace more focused verticals in three areas:

Target market. Of course, you want to work with everyone, because if the whole world is your market, you are unlimited in who you can serve. But it's a much stronger selling point when you can tell the companies in a given industry that you know their industry well.

Not long ago, I learned about a marketing firm that focused exclusively on serving personal injury lawyers. Not only did they limit themselves to the legal profession, they also limited themselves to a certain segment of the legal profession. They developed a system that was highly successful, and they offered exclusive representation for one firm in each city.

Who is the expert on serving the needs of banks? Of schools? Of manufacturers? Of construction companies? Of automotive companies? If you can develop a specialty based on your superior knowledge of a certain market — or just a few markets — you can own those markets. You can become almost impossible for a competitor to tangle with. You may be pursuing a market that's smaller than the whole world, but it should still be big enough to fill your capacity and give you room to grow.

Specialty. Many entrepreneurs want to be "full-service" shops, which means they bring lots and lots of functions under one roof. Yet how many things can you really be good at? Perhaps more importantly, how many things can you be the *best* at?

You can offer products or services that go together, but you should be careful not to become so unfocused that you're trying to sell things at which you don't excel. If you only make pillows, but you make the best pillows, there should be plenty of people who want what you're offering. If you only do digital data backup, but you have the most robust system anywhere, you will find high demand for your service. Specialize, and be the best. You'll become very difficult to compete with.

Geography. There's a whole world out there, and technology allows us to work with anyone these days. So why accept geographic limits to our market? One reason is that economies of scale don't always work when we go too far to find customers. I once had an opportunity to work with a client in Dubai. At first it seemed exciting, and the money they were offering wasn't bad at all. Then I started looking at the details of what would be required — the travel time, the fatigue, the attention drawn away from other clients, and the missed family time. I realized I wouldn't come out as far ahead as I thought. There are hidden costs to handling out-of-town business.

The hidden costs of handling business remotely vary from industry to industry. Some services can be handled with phone, video conferencing, and email. However, even then you must consider the cost of pursuing out-of-town business compared to focusing on a local area. There is a particular geographic area where you will do your best work. Once you identify it, that's where you need to focus.

I am not saying you should never, under any circumstance, work with someone who fits outside these verticals. Sometimes you're approached by a customer who's waving so much money — and whose demands are so attainable — you'd be a fool to say no. But when that happens, charge a premium.

You shouldn't knock yourself out pursuing business that is outside your verticals. Deal with it if it comes to you and make smart decisions about it. Maybe it makes sense and maybe it doesn't.

However, you *will* grow better if you stay within the limits of your verticals. That's because you are always going to do better work when you do the kind of work you do best, for the customers who are the best fits, and in the geographic area where you perform best.

Not all limits are limits on your success. Sometimes limits save you the trouble of drifting outside your areas of strength and put you in a position to be even more successful. I know that it's counterintuitive that limits can actually help you grow, but a lot of the best ideas are.

Wake-Up Call: As Pat Flynn said, "The riches are in the niches."[1]

23

STRUCTURE: EVEN IN THIS FAST AND LOOSE AGE, WE STILL NEED IT

You might have to be a certain age to notice this, but if you are, you definitely will: The world has become far less structured than it used to be. While that creates a lot of opportunities for entrepreneurs, it comes with some challenging implications, as well.

For the most part, structure has broken down because people like to be free from it. They like being able to work wherever and whenever they want. They also like being able to educate their kids from anywhere. They like being able to watch their TV shows and their movies on demand in their own environment. They like being able to access information at a moment's notice wherever they are and whatever they're doing.

It's probably hard for a person under 35 to relate to this, but it wasn't that long ago when this complete lack of structure was unthinkable. From the end of World War II through the mid-1990s, ours was a very structured society. Indeed, we built these structures in order to win WWII. It was one of the greatest achievements in the history of our society. Once the war was won and the soldiers came home, they blended right in, and Americans worked within that structure to produce astonishing results over the course of the next five decades.

The structural norms didn't change for a long time. We had our three TV networks. We had our local public schools. We had our home phone numbers and our six or seven local radio stations, and we knew we could get local news at 6:00 and national news at 6:30.

This was life in America for multiple generations, and the corporate world had its own familiar structure, with the 8-to-5 workday and the company hierarchy. A lot of this was because there was no other way to do it. It was efficient and productive, and most people learned to effectively work within this structure.

Yet, those structures, which made us so productive and efficient, arguably destroyed themselves. They did it by creating the technologies that rendered the old structures unnecessary. We wouldn't have remote workers, on-demand video, and real-time social media if the old structure hadn't invented the technologies that made them all possible.

Now that they're possible, we want all the unstructured freedom this new world can give us, and that's especially true of younger people – who have little or no memory of the old structured system and no concept of why they would want any part of it.

In a way, you can't blame them. Who wouldn't love the idea of making your own rules, your own hours, and your own methods of working? Who wouldn't want to enjoy the kind of freedom their parents and grandparents never even dreamed of?

However, there are downsides to the loss of structure, especially for young people, but also for businesses in general. Sometimes it's better for the human brain to operate within structure. There are times, places, and circumstances in which you can't just hope you're doing the right thing. Structure fills in those gaps.

That's especially true when it comes to process. Manufacturers know this well, although they're not the only ones: Documented processes are crucial to achieving consistent high-level performance. Corporations invest millions into training their people to learn their documented processes because it's essential to quality control.

It's easy to understand why structure is important on a shop floor, but it's a mistake to dismiss it in other business settings – even if we're talking about a small professional services firm.

Each business leader has to decide which elements of the business need structure and which ones can allow more flexibility. Maybe you want to be very firm about an 8-to-5 workday because your team dynamics depends on it. Maybe you can be a lot more flexible about how you manage things like vacation time, expense reimbursements, and employee reviews. However, if you're determined to always have everything unstructured, you're putting yourself at risk for a lot of problems.

For one thing, not everything is your decision. The IRS imposes some pretty inflexible requirements for how you do your accounting. That's structure imposed by Washington, D.C., and the IRS doesn't care that your employees like things loose. The same is true of OSHA and safety regulations.

Structure gives definition to things. It makes it possible for you to measure progress toward goals. It also makes it possible for you to quantify goals and identify problems. Without structure to guide your work process, your people can never be sure if they're doing what they should be doing, or how well they're doing it.

Structure is also useful for younger workers for another reason: Learning to discipline oneself is usually a long-term endeavor, and structure helps to define the discipline that is necessary. Many young people have dreams of running their own businesses. If they have no familiarity with the basic structure of a business, they won't have any idea what they need to build.

Granted, that young person may want to run a very unconventional business, with very loose operations that give a lot of autonomy to workers. I have no problem with anyone wanting to try that. Yet without understanding more conventional business structure as a baseline, how do you know how to apply the variations to make your unconventional idea work?

Learning to work within a structured environment teaches young people a lot about business and themselves. It may also inspire ideas for how they can do things better than the norm, and I applaud that. However, until you've functioned within such a structure, you're just guessing at what you think you might want to do.

Time marches on, and the technological innovations we've developed in the past 30 years have made it possible for us to do astonishing things. There's no reason the structure of business shouldn't evolve to take full advantage of these things. I am not in any way suggesting we should go back to the way we did things in 1945, or even in 1995.

Still, structure helps people and organizations succeed in ways you often don't appreciate until you make the mistake of trying to do business without it. No matter how technology and culture changes, we will always need structure to help make sense of it all.

> **Pro Tip:** Every business will have a different perspective on structure. You will have to decide where to have structure based on your needs and beliefs.

Wake-Up Call: Define which parts of your business must be structured and which parts can be unstructured.

24

BE PREPARED FOR THE POST-BHAG LETDOWN

I love Jim Collins's concept of the BHAG — the Big Hairy Audacious Goal.[1] I've been involved with three of them, two professional and one personal, and they're among the most important, memorable, and rewarding experiences I've ever had.

Not only were the pursuits of these BHAGs thrilling and challenging — the sort of thing from which you can't help but experience growth, but achieving them made a real impact. I'm glad I was part of them. I think everyone should pursue at least one BHAG.

However, I also want to warn you about something: The aftermath of the BHAG can turn into a real letdown — the sort of thing that might even cost you the people who were most instrumental in achieving the BHAG in the first place. Also, that letdown is not necessarily a bad thing, although you will probably not see it that way at the time.

The decision to chase a BHAG is a special event. It's the combination of a unique opportunity, a crucial need, and the right timing. You can't be chasing BHAGs all the time, because the point of the big goal is usually to set you up for a smoother and more sustainable path to success. At some point, you need to be finished with the BHAG and focus on turning the flywheel. (For more information on the flywheel, read the chapter "Whatever You Do, Don't Abandon the Flywheel.")

Sometimes you have to achieve a BHAG in order to get the flywheel to turn as it should, and when you're in the middle of that pursuit, there's nothing like it.

In 1998, I was hired as a network engineer for Cornerstone University, just months after the university president had embraced the BHAG of equipping every freshman at the school with a laptop. Of course, it wasn't simply a matter of buying laptops and handing them out. They needed to be customized. The school's IT infrastructure had to be seriously upgraded so it could function like a real network.

This was a massive undertaking, and I led it with a shoestring budget. We had to transform an assortment of completely antiquated technologies into a state-of-the-art network, in addition to acquiring all the laptops, unboxing them and configuring them.

The staff needed laptops, too, because everyone at the university had to be operating on the same system. In addition, everyone had to be educated about how to use this entirely new system. To make it all work, we had to rewire dorm rooms and classrooms.

It was a gigantic challenge. Looking back, I'm astonished we pulled it off in three years, but we did. We accomplished the BHAG. At that point, all I was expected to do was manage what we had built.

Within three months, I was looking for another job. Why? Was it because I didn't like my boss? The university's mission? My pay? My co-workers? The organizational culture?

No, no, no, no and no. I loved them all, and I still do. But after achieving that BHAG, the thought of just sitting there every day and acting as a caretaker over what we had built was not appealing to me. The entire experience of working there suddenly changed from a constant rush of challenges to a mundane day-to-day existence.

That was fine from the school's perspective. That's why we built the network, and it's exactly how we wanted it to run. If you're always chasing IT goals, you're not doing the primary thing people expect you to do, which in the case of Cornerstone University was educating students. The point of the BHAG was to enable simpler and better operations going forward, so someone in my position could simply function as a caretaker without having to deal with massive challenges all the time.

Except that I didn't want to be that person. I like massive challenges, and when you decide to pursue a BHAG, you need to bring people like that into your organization. They're just who you need at that point in time, and you're not very likely to accomplish a BHAG without them.

However, ongoing management of a robust system that's designed to largely run itself requires a different kind of person — one with just as much value as the serial BHAG-chaser. There's nothing at all wrong with having the ability to keep things running smoothly, even if no one really notices you're there. There's nothing wrong with finding satisfaction in such a role.

It's just that whoever fits that role is probably a different person from the BHAG-chaser, although it's not likely most organizations are going to see it that way in the moment. No one is going to hire someone to accomplish a big goal and then, upon their success, fire them. You would think the chance to live a quieter day-to-day life would be part of the reward of achieving the BHAG.

That's often not how it works. What follows the BHAG might be described as BHAG fatigue. If company leaders aren't careful, you could find your team suffering from lethargy that lasts for months. So, what do you do about it?

An easy temptation is to say: Let's pursue another BHAG! That is almost always a mistake. The reason you pursue a BHAG is that there's a strategic need for it, and a real advantage to accomplishing it. You don't chase a BHAG just for the sake of chasing a BHAG. And when you try, your people will quickly recognize that it's a contrived goal.

The best way to deal with the post-BHAG letdown is to be prepared for it. Some of the people who achieved the BHAG for you might stick around if you've presented them with a long-term picture of the company's plans — and how they fit in them. Some might enjoy their role in turning the flywheel every day.

However, being prepared also means not being gobsmacked if some of your key people leave and go looking for another company that needs to achieve another BHAG. It's the nature of some people — present company included. Use it as an opportunity to fill the role with someone more suited for what you'll need in the post-BHAG era.

You could have bigger problems than a well-conceived system that operates efficiently, along with the opportunity to find just the right people to run it for you. Just don't be too surprised when it happens.

Wake-Up Call: Be prepared for the BHAG-letdown you will feel when you achieve that ultimate goal. It's real and it happens.

25

THE LONG TAIL OF BUYING HAS MADE MARKETING SUPERIOR TO SALES

I t used to be that companies tried to make up for weak marketing with strong sales. For example, what did they do when they couldn't quantify their marketing efforts? They'd have their sales staff do more cold calls and schedule more meetings. At least they could quantify those.

However, the buying public has changed that approach to finding more business, in large part by giving us — over the past two decades — a phenomenon called the long tail of buying.

The long tail of buying increases your need for serious marketing. Let me explain more.

Marketing builds your brand — your reputation. It establishes who you are, what makes you different, and how people should identify you. It used to be said that Coke was established, and Pepsi was playful. Nordstrom's brand was associated with great customer service, while Kmart was known for low prices.

Of course, you'll recall, that eating Quaker Oats was the right thing to do because Wilford Brimley told you so.

It took substantial marketing work to establish these brand identities, and not a single sales call had anything to do with them. When you've got a massive marketing budget, you can invest a lot into building your brand. Yet even Coke and Pepsi weren't always massive corporations, so they had to invest a lot into building their brands during the years when their margins were still tight. The fact that they stuck with it is the reason their brands are so powerful today.

One of the longstanding problems with marketing, though, is that it was difficult to quantify the return on investment. So, when the vice president of sales and marketing is looking for a way to quantify his or her department's efforts, there's an easy temptation: Focus on sales calls! Just like that, sales becomes senior to marketing because it's the easiest fallback.

Today, though, consumers want to make their own purchase decisions without being contacted by a salesperson. They want to do their own product research. They want to check out reviews and other information pertaining to the reputation of the product or service and the company behind it.

That means you're not going to be rewarded for going to them. You have to get them to come to you, and the need to do that brings us back to marketing — that activity that frustrated you because you couldn't quantify the results.

I've got good news about your frustrations. Today, we have tools that yesterday's world didn't have to measure your marketing results, and the changing habits of buyers will work to your advantage if you stay focused on your marketing efforts.

Between World War II and the Dotcom boom of the late 1990s, there was an unmistakable trend in most industries: Three top brands tended to dominate. In retail it was Macy's, JCPenney, and Sears. In automotive it was General Motors, Ford, and Chrysler. In cereal it was Kellogg's, Post, and General Mills. The examples go on and on, and if we wanted to, we could fill the book with examples of the three-product giants in every industry prior to the Dotcom boom.

If you weren't one of the big three in most industries, you might still get a smattering of sales, but you would struggle to achieve a footing in the marketplace, let alone any sort of growth. There were a few exceptions, but this was the rule.

The Dotcom boom changed that. While most industries still saw three, four, or five major brands battling for market supremacy, consumers became a lot more willing to consider boutique offerings that had their own unique distinctions. The previous generation's insistence on the safe, established name gave way to a new willingness to take a chance and try something different.

This phenomenon became known as the long tail of buying. It has given niche competitors a chance where previously they would have had none.

What that means is that you no longer need to build brands as powerful as Coke and Pepsi to compete. Now, you just have to do a good job of being where the buyers are and being ready for them. If your marketing efforts can put you in that position, you can be part of the long tail of buying.

Tools are being rapidly developed that actually help you quantify the value of your marketing efforts. New products can evaluate the impact of email, social media marketing, direct marketing, and even traditional mail. These tools are giving marketers an unprecedented look at the performance of their efforts.

Just consider email marketing. Email has been around as a mainstream communication tool for more than 25 years, but in the early days there was no way to measure how effective a given email was. Now we can measure how many opens, how many clicks, and what kind of engagement a given email produces. We can also tailor emails to the specific data we have.

When you advertise on social media, you can get reports with a variety of different breakdowns that tell you who engages, where they're from and lots of other details.

It's more plausible than ever to measure your marketing efforts, and more crucial than ever that you prioritize them. So, if you are stuck in the old paradigm of needing to sell more, stop and think about how much investment you have made in your marketing efforts. The world has changed, and it is waiting for you to change with it.

Wake-Up Call: You are spending too much time and money on sales and too little on effective marketing.

PART III

EXECUTION

26

COMPANIES OFTEN WASTE GREAT TRAINING WITH BAD FOLLOW-UP

O ne of the most obvious challenges with training is choosing the right messenger to inspire change in people. If you're the boss, you may be one of the worst possible choices, simply because your people know you too well. It's hard to take that Superman cape seriously when you work every day with Clark Kent.

Your people know you — warts and all — and they may like you, but that doesn't mean you're the best person to impart the kind of training message that brings about the transformation you're looking for.

Even if you pick the right messenger, I often find that companies face a much bigger challenge where training is concerned — and it's a problem of their own making. People may be ready to embrace change, but when the training session is done, the organization isn't prepared to facilitate the change.

Often this is simply because the company does not plan for follow-up on the material presented in the training. Let's say you want people to be more proficient at using a certain system, so the training is focused on that. Or, let's say you want people to embrace a completely different philosophy when it comes to sales. So, you bring in a dynamite trainer who presses all their buttons, and your employees all buy into the idea.

That's great, but what will happen when training is over and they're back to their usual day-to-day tasks? Is the company going to spend time in the aftermath making sure the use of the new system or the new approach is fully incorporated into the company's processes?

I can tell you firsthand that I made this mistake year after year. Some years I would get excited about a new tool, technology, or system that I had found, and I would go back and try to train my staff on it. Eventually, I found out that doing the training myself didn't work, so I moved to hiring outside training. It helped a little, and more than anything it made me feel better about those training days. I want to emphasize that it felt good to do the training, but the reality is that we went back to our jobs and just did the same things.

I believe this happens because we get an emotional high — actual endorphins running through our bodies — from having top-notch trainers explain change that could radically transform our companies, but it doesn't solve the problems, unless team members actually implement the training.

Employees can also get very excited about an idea or a direction during a training session. They can come out of the training session pumped up to get going on what they've learned. They can be convinced that their work experience will never be the same because of it, but what happens if they find their work experience is exactly the same as it was before?

What happens if they return to their offices or cubicles and find the same familiar tasks are piling up? What if their pile of work is even higher because they just missed a day of work for training?

Now it's a matter of trying to dig out from under the pile, and before many days have gone by, they're starting to forget what had them so excited during that training session. They're starting to wonder if the company wants them to do what they just spent time learning. They're starting to wonder if there would be any reward for doing so.

This is usually because the company failed to plan how to implement the training. The company brought in the trainer because there's a fundamental belief in the power of training, but no one thought about what would come next.

They could have invested in digital accountability systems, or some new software, or even just an app that would have kept the priorities identified in training on target. It could be as simple as having a manager touch base with employees to make sure they're making progress on what they learned.

Any follow-up is better than none, but the best approach is to preplan a comprehensive effort to implement what the trainers teach. That's not only about time. It's also about commitment of resources, support, and accountability.

If the employees who are now embracing change come back to a system that hasn't changed, the system will reject the very change you paid the trainers to teach. They need to see that leadership is committed to the change, and that this is reflected in their tangible responsibilities. They need to see that they will be rewarded if they make the changes. They also need to know they will be held accountable if they don't.

Often, a company with problems thinks it can solve the problems just by investing in training or consulting. But that's not the solution. The solution is to know what will work better and commit to it. Then bring in the trainers to make sure the team is equipped to embrace the change.

The trainers aren't going to make things different. You are. Unless you don't.

Wake-Up Call: Training is good. However, execution on the training is far better.

27
_____

BUSINESS LEADERS ARE OFTEN BLINDSIDED BY EMPLOYEE RESISTANCE TO CHANGE

_____

L eaders are constantly surprised when employees are resistant to change. This negative reaction to change is a phenomenon that repeats itself in the business world, and yet it *constantly* surprises business leaders when it happens.

I was a perfect example of this. At a minimum, once a year, and sometimes once a quarter, I would lock myself in my office and come up with an idea for a very big change. I was excited about the change and couldn't wait to tell everyone at the company how great it would be.

I would call an all-hands meeting and introduce my new idea. I'd watch with great anticipation for the excitement on the faces of the employees, but their faces were filled with dread instead.

Like many leaders, I was stunned, having been sure everyone would love the change. But they didn't. With this being so predictable, it's hard to understand why leaders are so often blind-sided by it. However, I think it's mainly due to the one fact that separates the change-driving leader from the change-resisting employees: No one likes changes that were someone else's ideas. That's hard to accept when the ideas were yours, and you think they're great.

Change imposed by someone else seems threatening to people, as people tend to be comfortable with the status quo. They may not love the status quo. However, over time they learn how to manage the familiar, and they don't like having that comfort yanked away from them for something that's allegedly better.

Also, if we're to be honest, we should recognize that most businesses encourage people to stay inside the status quo as much as possible. Making things. Selling things. We reward people when they master their status quo. We don't encourage them to break out of it.

Some of the management philosophies we learned from Japan, like Lean and Kaizen, seek to reward people for driving positive change — even if it means more automation or reductions of motion. People are naturally resistant to those things because they appear on the surface to make the people less necessary. Yet, these systems reward them for helping to make such changes happen.

That is not the day-to-day thinking of your average manager, so you can understand why people have a hard time feeling confident a big change will benefit them.

More fundamentally, people don't like change when they don't have a voice in it. It's understandable that a business leader who comes up with an exciting idea can't wait to share it with everyone. However, to the rest of the team, it feels like something that's being imposed on them.

Now I am not saying every decision a business leader makes needs to be made via consensus of the entire team. You can't operate that way. It would cripple you. However, when you've got a big idea that will fundamentally affect everyone, you'd be smart to listen to everyone. You might even learn some things that would make your idea better.

That seems like such an obvious principle of management — people resist changes when they weren't part of the decision-making process. It's hard to work out why business leaders are so consistently blindsided by it. Part of it might have to do with the science of the brain. When people think they have a good idea and they feel excited about it, that releases dopamine and drives a feeling of euphoria. It's hard to imagine when you're feeling this way that everyone won't feel the same. And that makes it all the more deflating when the staff's response to your big idea is, "What?" Leaders are optimistic, and no one has a clearer picture than they do of their own visions. Some of them, especially if they're still new in business, may have never encountered serious resistance to one of their ideas. There are ways you can avoid that resistance, and they're not that complicated.

The first, and most obvious, is to get input from key players before you simply spring it on everyone. This will allow you to vet your idea and make sure it can stand up to scrutiny. It will allow you to receive information that can help you improve the idea, and it will make key players feel like they had a part in the process.

When you present the idea, you shouldn't present it in a top-down sort of way, making people feel that it's being imposed on them. You might present a direction you're thinking of and ask people for their ideas for how to get there, rather than just inform them you've got the whole plan already worked up.

You might need to press pause on your idea when you hear from people, because even if you're 100 percent convinced it's great, you're never going to get great results if you are fighting with your team.

Sometimes resistance helps you. Sometimes it uncovers bad implementation. Sometimes you have to give an idea time and let it develop at the right pace, rather than trying to make it happen too quickly while people worry that it's not going to go well for them.

Maybe you've got an idea for a new service, and you want to make it happen right away. However, you don't really know how to perform that service yet, and it's better to take time to learn before you start promising everyone that you can do it immediately. Your employees will respect you, and you'll be better off, if you exercise such wisdom.

Change has to be sold, but the key to successful change is not just the sales job. It's also understanding how to make your team part of the change, so they know you're looking out for them rather than just championing your big idea.

An important parallel concept that we need to make sure we highlight before turning you loose is that your staff are not mind readers. Too often, once a leader communicates a change, he or she forgets to communicate all the details. Often, the details need to be communicated more than once. In my coaching practice, I've had a chance to see this multiple times. A leader has a great new vision, gets buy in, communicates it well, but forgets that most of the details are in his or her head. As a result, the execution is never what the leader imagined.

Execution and communication must run on parallel tracks to make sure that the idea is executed as you envisioned.

Wake-Up Call: Don't just announce big ideas. Collaborate on big ideas.

28

FIRST THINGS FIRST: HOW YOU START ANYTHING IS CRUCIAL TO SUCCESS

The next time you decide to do something — whether it's the pursuit of a client, the hire of a new employee, or the development of a new product — chances are the success or failure of that endeavor will be largely determined right at the start.

That's because how you start anything you do is important, and most people would readily nod their heads in agreement. Yet, in my experience, far too many people don't start these major initiatives well at all.

They don't think things through. They don't plan, and they don't challenge themselves with difficult questions. They're driven by excitement, impatience, or too much passion for a particular idea. All they want to do is get it going as quickly as they can.

The temptation to start something, without getting it right, can result from a number of things. One is impatience. A few years ago, I was working toward a sizeable transaction. It was going to have major implications for the company I was working for at the time, and also for me financially. I wanted so badly to get it done, but it seemed to me that the transaction had come to a near stop, and it was driving me crazy. I felt like I just needed to take some sort of step to make something happen, but there didn't seem to be a step to take.

Finally, I called my attorney. I told him I just wanted an hour to talk to him about all this, and that I didn't even care if he billed me. He listened patiently, and then gave me some of the best advice I've ever gotten from a human being. He said he understood it seemed at that moment like it was taking forever. However, in the long term I would look back on this, and it would seem like it had been a quick process. He cautioned me to be careful about short-circuiting the process rather than letting it play out as it should.

He was right. In retrospect, it does seem like it happened quickly, and I'm very glad I let the process play out because the outcome was much better as a result. Yet, in the moment, we so often want to get the outcome instantaneously, and we're not willing to go through the process that's required to make the outcome the best it could or should be.

Another reason for poor outcomes is that many in the business world are embracing a weird misapplication of Thomas Edison's quote: "I have not failed. I've just found 10,000 ways that won't work."[1] This quote helped bring support for the "fail fast" concept. Edison encouraged people to fail fast and fail often, by which he meant two things: First, don't waste a bunch of time on a concept that's not going anywhere. Second, don't be so afraid of failure that you aren't willing to take risks. All of that is sound thinking.

However, it's not good to rush an idea before it is ready, and then when it's not working, pull the plug on it quickly, only to pat yourself on the back for "failing fast." That is not the idea. The wisdom of "fail fast" is that you don't get bogged down in something that's not going anywhere, because failure isn't the objective. Success is. Before you start anything, it's essential to make sure you've got a good foundation in place, and that you're willing to take the time that's necessary to get it right.

If you fail fast, you still failed! No, you shouldn't be afraid of that because failure is inevitable in life. However, there's a difference between not being afraid of it and not doing what you can do to prevent it. If that's how you approach things, you deserve no credit for failing fast. You accomplish nothing positive or productive by doing that, and remember, positive and productive accomplishments are the idea. If you insist on following the "fail fast" mantra, would you please read the chapter "Fire Bullets, Then Cannonballs" in *Great by Choice*?[2] I personally believe this is a much more positive way of looking at experimentation in business rather than the "fail fast" philosophy.

Another reason we sometimes don't start things correctly is that we're too invested in an idea. A new employee will be amazing and turn your whole enterprise around. A prospective new client will change everything to set you up to double your revenue. That product brainstorm you had at 3:00 in the morning is so cool, and everyone you talk to about it (which is pretty much everyone) thinks so. You've got to get it on the market yesterday!

You're so convinced this is going to be the biggest turning point of your life, you almost don't want to think it through critically. That might force you to ask tough questions about it, and you've already made up your mind that you're in love with it.

That's not good. If an idea is solid, it will stand up to scrutiny. If it's a good idea but it has some flaws, scrutiny will help to correct those flaws so you can launch it and make it work over the long term. If all you're trying to do is rush it out of the box, you're much more likely to end up telling people, "Hey, at least I failed fast!"

Even ideas that are well thought-through and planned out can still end up having flaws, but the stronger you start, the better the chance you can pivot and still achieve success. Maybe you hire a person, and it turns out the person isn't quite the fit you expected for the responsibilities you had in mind. However, because you did your due diligence, you know this is a very strong person. So, you can pivot to a different position, and you can still get an amazing employee out of it.

Pivots can work, but they have to follow a solid start in which you asked the right questions, allowed processes to play out, and developed a solid plan for success.

Entrepreneurs, I am talking to you. I know you love to rush in, and you are eager to get to the outcome. I understand that. But without a strong start, the outcome is not going to be what you want. Take a step back, do it right, and start off on solid footing. You will wait a little longer for the outcome you wanted, but I promise you the wait will be more than worth it.

Wake-Up Call: A rushed start will lead to rushed outcomes, but not necessarily good outcomes.

29

HOW TO KEEP YOUR ORGANIZATIONAL CHART FROM SLIPPING INTO A DOOM LOOP

I n my business, Red Wagon Advisors, I talk to my clients about doom loops, and I apply the concept to many different situations. In this chapter, I'm applying it specifically to a company's organizational chart, because there's an all-too-common pattern you'll see with company leaders that traps them in such a loop. If you recognize this pattern, because you've seen it in your own company, do whatever you have to in order to break free from a doom loop.

What is a doom loop? Let me give you an example. The doom loop usually begins because a director or middle management-type person leaves the company. The person above whomever is leaving decides, at least for the moment, not to fill the position but to step in and do the job.

This is not the worst thing to do for a short period of time. You don't want to rush into an important hire, and there's some value to executive leadership being familiar with what certain jobs require.

However, trouble can set in quickly. The executive has been doing the additional job for a while now and shows no inclination to let go and to hire someone. Then another person leaves, and the same executive leader figures he can absorb the duties of that job too.

It's not hard to understand what makes this tempting. Obviously, you save money if you wait on filling that spot. Plus, when you do the job yourself, it gets done the way you want it done. Theoretically, anyway.

It's easy to see why this becomes such a doom loop for a company. A loop is something that keeps repeating itself — and that you can never seem to escape. The executive who keeps trying to do these jobs is in exactly such a loop, trying to be Superman and performing all these roles. The executive thinks by putting lots of time into it, or by drawing on professional experience, or perhaps by the sheer force of will, that he or she can perform all the jobs.

Yet, inevitably, the executive is going to get bogged down in the muck of these roles and will not be leading. Every organization thrives on leadership, and team members count on leaders who are available and engaged at the leadership level.

The team members will sense when you're not leading and engaged. They will recognize that this particular leader is so often bogged down with a multitude of tasks, it's no longer fruitful or plausible to look to him in a leadership role. He won't tell them not to, but his demeanor will.

In the meantime, none of these jobs are getting done the way they're supposed to. Therefore, the company won't perform at an optimal level, losing customers and revenue. Now there is even less money available than there was before to fill these positions.

This is why we call it a doom loop. You don't have enough people in crucial positions, and it's hurting your performance and costing you money.

Sometimes this is the result of a setback, and it starts with an attempt to save money. Other times it results from growth. The company adds a facility or a territory, and instead of hiring people to run those territories or facilities, a top executive gets the idea that he or she can do it. This is the best way to jeopardize that growth you've worked so hard to achieve.

So how do you get out of this loop? It starts with that one executive (or more if that's your reality) who can't accept that it's not his job to do other people's jobs for them. You must recognize that this is inhibiting your growth because you can't grow if you don't have a strong enough team to sustain it.

Leaders have to be present, and they're not present when they're distracted trying to do someone else's job. They're not focused on leadership. They're trying to serve two masters, and they're not pleasing either one of them.

Now I recognize that it's sometimes necessary to collapse roles. Sometimes a company takes a financial downturn, and it has to let some people go, which requires others to take on additional responsibilities.

If that's the case, then collapse that role so it's manageable by a person who's taking it on as an additional responsibility. However, that's not what we're talking about here. We're talking about situations in which the role remains every bit as big and complicated as it's always been. However, someone who should know better insists on taking on a second role full-bore — in addition to the leadership functions that person has already been assigned and should be focusing on.

I've seen doom loops like this in many companies. It's easy to fall into them and hard to get out; however, you can do it by making the decision to put the right people in the right positions — one at a time. Tell your leaders their job is to lead, and let the people handle the tasks that are waiting along the line. Be consistent about maintaining enough staff to keep your performance and growth strong. Once you get into that loop, it's very hard to get out.

Wake-Up Call: You seem like a hero when you are doing someone else's work. However, you're the villain — making it difficult to sustain growth.

30

IN YOUR COMPANY, RULES ARE THE LAST THING THAT SHOULD BE UNWRITTEN

The idea of a corporation's "core values" became popular with the 2001 publishing of Jim Collins's iconic book *Good to Great*.[1] Collins was so eloquent in presenting the idea, that "core values" largely replaced the old corporate mission statement as a company's defining identity.

I believe in having core values that are clearly stated and used as the basis for day-to-day operations, but there's a problem. Core values can only go so far in establishing the policies by which a company needs to operate. Over the course of the past several decades, it's become unpopular to have formal corporate policies in writing — on everything from work hours to attire to whether people work at desks.

No one wants to be the rigid fuddy-duddy who hands down all the rules. Formal corporate policies have a 1960s feel to them (and I'm talking the very conservative corporations of the '60s, not the flower children out in the streets). With the emergence of the hip dot-com companies and the growth of the Silicon Valley culture, the trend has been toward a much more laid-back, live-and-let-live type of work setting. Throw COVID into the mix, and we are in a very relaxed and unstructured business environment.

Theoretically, this is employee-friendly, because no one is telling you what you have to do or how you have to do it. It's all about results, because along the way you're just free to be you and do your thing, though there are problems with that.

Let me use an example to illustrate the problem of a company that doesn't have specific policies. Recently, the daughter of one of my friends showed up at work wearing black lipstick, and this is the same place where she has worked for nearly a decade. She's had the same boss the entire time, and she's worn the black lipstick on multiple occasions without anyone raising an objection.

However, on this day, her boss didn't like what he saw. So, he told my friend's daughter that she needed to take the black lipstick off because it was inappropriate for the work setting.

Now the point here is not to argue about whether black lipstick is or is not professional. The point is that, absent any clear policy on the subject, it all became about her boss's opinion (or her boss's *mood* on that given day).

The fact of the matter is that there *are* rules, even if you don't write them down. The *unwritten* rules arise from the company's employee culture, or from the opinions of influential people. Maybe you don't have a mandatory start time in the morning, but it's common for people to show up at 8:30. If you show up at 9:30, you're not violating a policy, but you're running afoul of the culture. You might be doing a perfectly fine job, but you're still giving yourself a problem you don't need.

When you leave the rules unwritten, several bad things happen. One is that you lose control of who makes the rules — and believe me, someone will make them. Another is that some people will know the rules better than others. The plugged-in people, who are close to the influential people, will have a better sense of what they can and can't do than those who are shy or on the social outskirts of the company. The employees who regularly go out for food or drinks together after work are going to be more attuned to the unwritten rules than the people who go straight home to their families, or who go work out.

As we saw from our black lipstick example, employees don't know how to follow the rules if you're letting people make them up as they go along.

You do need some policies, and I understand that companies don't want to follow the strict, rigid model of generations past. So, I suggest a particular way of doing this. It involves four columns you create.

The first column, on the very far left, lists your core values. These should be three-to-five key statements that define the principles and beliefs that guide your company.

The second column is for specific rules you make. Is there a standard start time for work? Are neck tattoos okay? Does everyone have to work at a desk? How can flex time be used? Are you allowed to swear? *Are you allowed to wear black lipstick?* If you think it's important to be clear about an issue, this is where you make it official.

The third column is called "Rules I Didn't Make." This involves best practices and industry standards that aren't so much your preference as they are norms for your profession. For example, it's standard for attorneys to wear suits to work. It's standard for food- service employees to wash their hands before preparing meals. It's standard for baseball players to wear uniforms, gloves, and caps. You may or may not agree with the rules you didn't make, but the point is to let employees know these rules apply because of the nature of your work.

The fourth column comes from an idea introduced by Patrick Lencioni, which is that of aspirational values.[2] These are ideas where you might fall short, but you aspire to them, nonetheless. For example, you might aspire to never make a mistake when taking care of clients. Now you're human, so you're going to make some mistakes, but you should still aspire to be impeccable in your work. Or, you might aspire to be professional at all times in your appearance and behavior. Chances are you're going to slip up at some point, but this is a worthy ideal to which you can aspire. So, the aspirational values are important, not because people will get fired if they fall short (they won't), but because you want them to know this is what they should be shooting for.

Finally, there's the question of things you can't anticipate. Some years back, when beards were less acceptable than they are now, I was getting ready to take an employee to a client meeting, and I thought he looked unacceptably scruffy. I didn't want him to go see the client looking like that. However, I had no policy defining "scruffy." It was just what my gut told me. This wasn't a good idea. So, I asked him to shave.

Now, he could have said, "There's no policy on scruffy!" And he would have been right. However, in this moment, I needed him to listen to me. Fortunately, he did.

For leaders, this is where your emotional bank account with your employees becomes so important. If you've consistently treated them with fairness, respect, and integrity, then you're a lot more likely to get their cooperation when the moment comes when you have to ask them to do something not governed by policy. This is important because there's no way you can anticipate everything that could ever come up, and sometimes you just have to use your own instincts.

If you're the kind of boss who has always been good to your people and always had their backs, you'll probably get their buy-in when you need them to shave, or change their clothes, or maybe even wash off the black lipstick.

Wake-Up Call: Every company has rules. The most unfair rules are the unwritten ones.

31

BUILDING COMMUNITY: I SHOULD HAVE RECOGNIZED THE VALUE SOONER

I've always been pretty comfortable taking a go-it-alone approach to things. It allows me to do things my way and follow my own priorities.

However, I've realized from looking back on my career that, too often, I missed an opportunity. I didn't seize the moment to build community.

You might think I'm simply going into Networking 101 here, but it's more than that. Anyone can show up at the Chamber of Commerce mixers or join the industry association group, and there's value to doing that. However, I'm talking more about seizing the opportunity when the chance to build community comes to you.

Consider the scenario in which one of your kids gets involved with scouting. You attend some of the meetings — maybe as a leader, maybe just as a parent. But you're surrounded by all kinds of people you could be connecting with. Do you connect with them? You're there anyway. Do you introduce yourself?

Or maybe you belong to a church. Do you walk in at the start of the service and walk out at the end of it? Or do you get involved with serving? And if you do that, do you make high-value connections with the people who serve alongside you? Do you find out what you can learn from those who are there? I am certainly not suggesting you go to church to make business contacts. What I'm saying is, if you're there anyway, why not take the opportunity to build community?

I used to find this very unnatural. I would go to events that were supposed to be for networking, and I would not get a lot out of it. This is not because I'm a shy person. Far from it. Making contacts in this way seemed awkward and unappealing.

Then I realized that I could be seizing so many opportunities. Just about everywhere you go could be a chance to build community. It's simply a matter of interacting with people and finding out who they are, what they do, and what they know.

I started building community in places people never even thought of. Once, at an industry trade show, I spent considerable time interacting with competitors. Now you might ask, why would I do that? Aren't you competing for customers? Sure, but you also find out from those conversations that you use a lot of the same suppliers as your competition, and there's value in building community around that.

Of course, when you allow your competitors to learn from you, it might make them better. There's nothing wrong with that. If your team is in a division where everyone is good, that's good for business and good for fan interest. It also keeps you sharper because you know you have to be your best at all times. I'm happy to have my competitors learn from me, and, of course, I learn back.

One of the earliest lessons in this regard came more than 20 years ago when I decided to take a course to become a certified Microsoft engineer. I invested a lot of money in this course, and I borrowed most of it.

It will sound funny today, but back in the late 1990s, the class got most excited by the introduction of concepts like the MP3 and the Winamp. Music you could download? Listen to without a CD? What?

When a student shared this discovery, we quickly became

animated, and soon almost the entire class was sharing thoughts, ideas, and insights. By the end of that class, I'd learned more about Microsoft and engineering from those discussions shared among students than I had learned from any class session, and it was all because we built community. People got engaged with one another and turned the mere presentation of facts into a stimulating conversation.

This was a powerful moment of building community. It's the principle of the hive mind, which recognizes that we all learn more when we learn together. I should have learned this lesson sooner and applied it to my business. However, in recent years I've applied this concept well.

Remember, you don't have to go out of your way to do this. You can build community in the normal course of your life. When I find myself in a space where I can see there is value to be found in community-building, I go at it like a madman.

If you don't have a natural or obvious situation for building community, there are things you can do. You can join entrepreneur groups, mentoring organizations, or networking groups.

However, the key is to resolve to do it anywhere and everywhere you go. You can always interact with people, and you can always find value in doing that.

There's so much value to building community, and there are so many ways to do it. Just don't let too much time go by while you fail to realize the value of it.

Wake-Up Call: Entrepreneurs have an inclination to go it alone. If that's you, find a way to disrupt that inclination. You must build community and find support.

32

PUT IT – DON'T 'GET IT' – IN WRITING

There's a piece of advice you often get in business. You might have even gotten it from your dad at some point. It's bad advice, but it contains the seeds of something better. This ill-begotten advice is: "Get it in writing."

This is the refrain of the cynical fellow who's sure you're going to get screwed on every commitment someone makes to you. "Get it in writing" is designed as a failsafe that will force people to deliver on their promises, whether they want to or not.

It misses the mark, but that's not because putting agreements in writing is a bad thing. Far from it. The problem is with who's taking the initiative — or not taking it.

So, what's my problem with "get it in writing"? Simple: You don't want to get it in writing. You want to put it in writing rather than relying on the other party to do so.

I'm all about agreements being in writing. In fact, I'm appalled by how often people rely entirely on a verbal understanding. There are a number of reasons people do this, and it usually amounts to people trying to be too clever. The most common is that people think it gives them "flexibility" if they keep things up in the air. Once you've got an agreement in writing, they figure, you're limited to the written terms. If you stick with the handshake, you can always play fast and loose, and maybe you can take things in a different direction should one become appealing to you.

That's a big mistake. Putting what you've agreed to in writing doesn't mean you can't go back and add something later. Failing to do so, by contrast, plants the seeds of all kinds of misunderstandings. Another reason people don't put things in writing is that they lack confidence. You can't believe you got the client to agree to work with you, and you're scared to death to push it by actually asking for a signature on a document.

That, of course, tempts fate in a big way. If they believe in what they have agreed to, they'll sign the agreement. If they don't, you're better off finding out when they balk at a written agreement as opposed to doing two- or three-months' worth of work, only to find out that your invoices aren't going to be paid.

You absolutely want the agreement in writing. It clarifies what was agreed to and provides a perfect opportunity to smooth out any misunderstandings. It lays out clearly what each side expects of the other, and what will be required of each side to achieve the goals.

When you put something in writing, it also spells out the goals, which is more important than you might think. It's amazing how many times two parties make a deal and don't actually see eye-to-eye on why they're making the deal.

It makes no sense to wait on the other party to take the initiative when you could do it yourself. Putting it in writing and asking the other party to review and agree to the document is an opportunity for you to make clear how things are supposed to go. It's also a way to ensure that everyone will be fully engaged in the process of working together.

I saw a situation recently that illustrated this very well. A friend of mine joined a company that was growing, and he thought he could help them add new clients and reach an important growth goal. As an incentive, they promised him 15 percent of the company if he pulled in the numbers the two sides had agreed to.

However, no one put it in writing. That became an issue as months dragged on, and my friend started to question whether his bosses would come through with the shares they had promised him in the event he made his goal.

Eventually, he become so concerned he basically checked out for an entire summer and accomplished nothing. The company wasn't getting the growth it expected, and my friend wasn't getting any closer to his desired reward because he doubted it would be there for him.

Was he right to suspect the company would not honor its commitment? I don't know. Maybe he was on to something, or maybe he just jumped to conclusions from signals he was getting or wasn't getting from the bosses. What I do know is this: If the agreement had been in writing, he would have at least known he had solid legal standing.

In fact, verbal agreements are enforceable in most states, but for obvious reasons that's a much more complicated proposition than enforcing a written agreement. Enforcing a verbal agreement requires witnesses, and even then it's impossible to say that everyone will remember having heard the same thing.

My friend would have been better off with the deal in writing, but he shouldn't have "gotten it in writing." He should have put it in writing himself — with the help of an attorney if he felt the need — and presented it to the company to be signed. This would have given him first mover's advantage, the advantage of going first and anchoring the agreement to what he believed they verbally agreed to.

The leader of a serious, trustworthy company would absolutely sign a document formalizing the promise it had made. An untrustworthy person would save the other party a lot of time and aggravation by refusing to sign, thus proving the deal isn't for real and the envisioned work isn't worth doing. Along the way, the agreement you put in writing makes it clear to everyone what's expected. It also saves everybody a lot of time because if you're not willing to sign it, why even get started?

So, don't just keep things based on a handshake because you think it gives you flexibility. You've always got flexibility to make an adjustment if it works for everyone. Also, don't "get it in writing," because that means you're giving all the power to the other party.

Put it in writing. Do it yourself. And do it with confidence, because if you're as good as you told them you are when you got them to shake your hand, then they'll soon be very glad they signed that document and gave themselves the opportunity to work with you.

> If you've ever sat in a meeting with me, you'll notice I take notes. I like sending summaries to others in the meetings. It's not that I enjoy taking notes. I do it for the reasons listed in this chapter and because it gives me power in the conversation. For all these reasons, I put it in writing.

Wake-Up Call: Never get it in writing. Always put it in writing.

33

WHITEBOARDING BEST PRACTICES

When Bill Gates retired from Microsoft, he did a lot of interviews — and even a Netflix series called *Inside Bill's Brain*.[1] There are so many things we can learn from him, positive and negative! He had a think week twice a year where he went away by himself to read and think about new ideas for the company.[2] By the way, every CEO should do that. Being away helps you spot the next trends and grow your business.

One of the throwaway comments he made in an interview stuck with me. He mentioned that the whiteboard was one of the number one tools in his career.[3] That comment still influences me today.

Why do whiteboards work so well? We are only a few generations from humans who wrote on the walls. Further back, we are only a few thousand years from cave painters. It is hard wired into us to paint on walls. It's only in the last few decades that we have been using Excel, email, and spreadsheets. Writing on whiteboards works with the hard wiring of our brains. Plus, it provides interaction that is hard for even expensive technologies to match.

In the office, I recommend that everyone should have white-boards from floor to ceiling. Put whiteboards wherever you can. You can even have whiteboards painted on the wall. There are endless tips on how to best use a whiteboard. You can find them on the internet or in books, but here are my tips.

First, have as many whiteboards as possible to capture ideas. Why should you have so many? While writing ideas on one whiteboard, you may get another idea about a different topic. Go write it on another board. Stencil out the idea before you forget it. Our brain often produces multiple ideas at once, and we need to capture them before they disappear.

Second, our brains work best when we are standing, not sitting. It's easier for the brain to get that oxygen-rich blood. If you able to stand, install the whiteboard in a such a way that it makes it easy to use when you are on your feet.

Third, you must have dry-erase markers in multiple colors. Black markers are best for the bulk of your points and to make an outline. Concepts should also be marked in black. Blue markers are great for new ideas. It's like the blue ocean; it's the next destination where you could go. Epiphanies should also be in blue.

Green should be used for costs and anything that involves money. If you are looking for costs, money, expenses, or revenues, you can find it easily, if you mark it in green. You should always do your financial numbers in green. Red is always for something negative, unless it's Red Wagon or Redegades, which are two of my businesses. If there is something that could be a problem, mark it in red. It's a red flag.

Pro Tip: With few exceptions, don't get cute and use other colors.

Fourth, practice writing on the whiteboard and looking back at your audience. You should alternate between writing and talking. You must remember to do this. You don't talk to the whiteboard with your butt shaking to your audience behind you. People may forgive poor spelling, but they won't forgive you talking to the whiteboard.

Fifth, practice good penmanship. We all get in a hurry, but make your presentation look neat. Practice the pictures you will use in presentations. If you are working on an internet-based business, practice your clouds and firewalls. If you're in a financial business, practice drawing a spreadsheet. There are little techniques you can learn and plenty of free drawing videos on the web. You can look like more of an expert when you have the ability to draw and display good penmanship. My friend and colleague, Matt Reid, has the best white board penmanship skills I've ever seen. We used to sell technology together and do similar presentations. I have no data to back up this claim, but I have no doubt he closed more business based on his ability to draw and his penmanship on the white board.

> **Pro Tip:** Get off the PowerPoint and go to the whiteboard. You will have better sales and better buy-in from customers and employees.

Some people talk about TVs as alternatives to whiteboards. As of 2021, I have not found a big TV screen I can write on and be satisfied.

However, there are great whiteboard alternatives — the iPad Pro, Microsoft Surface, and Microsoft Surface Studio 2. These digital technologies are alternatives, and Microsoft Surface Studio 2 is worth the money. I use the Microsoft Surface Studio 2 in my practice daily.

How about painting your walls instead of buying whiteboards? If you decide to paint your walls with whiteboard paint, go floor to ceiling. Half-way doesn't look good. Also, put the paint on thick, and have it put on by a pro. Although it's expensive, not doing it well is even more expensive. With a painted whiteboard, you have to erase it almost immediately, if you want it to remain pristine and usable.

There are alternatives out there, but I prefer to have glass whiteboards that are magnetic. You can use magnets with them. Then you can add printed material to your whiteboard with magnets.

Pro Tips: Lysol wipes are hands down the best way to clean a white board. They work better than any EXPO spray or eraser. Also, if people accidentally take a Sharpie to a white board, write over it with a white board marker, and, in most cases, it will come off.

Wake-Up Call: We are all just cave painters using white boards.

PART IV

SALES/CASH

34

SHARKS ARE IN THE WATER: WILL YOU BE ONE OF THEM OR THEIR PREY?

———

There are sharks in the water. If you're in business in the 2020s, there's no escaping that. The only question is whether you're one of them – or if you're their prey.

In a decade like the 2020s, a lot of businesses are in precarious positions. They might have made questionable decisions for years, but good economic conditions allowed them to escape major consequences for a time. In a decade like this, your weaknesses get exposed, and you sometimes find yourself in a position where you can't refuse any offer that gives you an escape hatch.

That's where the sharks come in. There are always people looking for good bargains on businesses. They want your property. They want your fixtures. They want access to your clients. They probably have the ability to shore up the operation in ways that you can't, and they know you're not in a position to turn down their offer.

So, they're looking to buy, at a price that's very favorable to them. They're sharks, and I mean that without the slightest hint of condemnation. There's a reason sharks rule the ocean. They're a crucial part of the ecosystem, and it wouldn't work without them.

Sharks in business are doing what smart people always do. They're responding rationally to incentives. If a business is in precarious shape because it doesn't have a good balance sheet, or it hasn't been keeping its numbers as it should have, or it can't seem to make its cash flow work, the shark takes notice of these critical points.

The shark also knows that the assets of that business are probably worth more than its current leadership. Better leadership could turn it around. Sharks only want to make a minimal investment in a business like this because a) its performance doesn't justify any more than that, and b) the owner wouldn't be smart to hold out for any more than that.

So, I'm talking to the people who own businesses that might be targets of the sharks. How do you recognize these sharks? Often, they have made their money by coming into generational wealth or have gotten their money somehow on the sidelines. They don't want to build a business. They want to take over one that someone else has built but is having trouble leading to prosperity.

These sharks could invest in a business for a multiple on EBITA, which is the kind of business acquisition you'd hope to be part of if you're the seller. However, the sharks don't want to do that. They want to take on distressed businesses that they can get for mere book value, or maybe just the straight value of the assets and the cash on hand. In some cases, they'll want to take over your business, but they won't offer any more than to cover your payroll for the coming year.

That's quite a bargain, wouldn't you say? Acquiring all a company's assets just for keeping people employed?

These sharks have long memories. They know that in 2001, when we experienced the last recession similar to the current one (in other words, not precipitated by a financial market meltdown like in 2008), a lot of businesses changed hands for very little money.

Do you want to avoid being prey for sharks like this? Then do the following:

First, look at your cash conversion cycle, or CCC. That seems so fundamental. No one should even need to be told to do it, right?

But you have to tell NBA players to practice their free throws because they don't like to. I know better than to assume that everyone in business does this. Very few look at the full maturity of their CCCs. (For more details about CCC, read the "Cash" section in *Scaling Up*.)[1] Business owners usually just look at how quickly they can get one portion of that cycle back by collecting on current receivables.

However, you need to look at the full cash conversion cycle from top to bottom. Here are some questions to ask as you look at your cash conversion cycle: How do you get sales? How do you make things or deliver services more quickly? How can you collect the money faster? At the other end, how do you stretch your payables as long as possible without being unethical about it? If you don't have this mastered, you are ripe for a shark to come and get you.

Another solution is the "Power of One," which is discussed in *Scaling Up*.[2] You want to look at the seven key financial levers that you can influence to achieve more corporate success, such as increasing price, volume, and the number of days to pay creditors.[3] You also want to consider decreasing overhead, stock days, cost of goods sold, and length of time to collect money from clients.[4] If you're not inspecting every one of these in your weekly management meetings, you're in trouble.

Finally, you need to be in frequent and good communication with your bank. There has rarely been a time when the business community has had more access to capital than it does right now. If you're not talking to your banker, you could be missing out on an opportunity to either save or expand your business.

Now let's say you're on top of all this. Your finances are sound, and your performance is solid. In this case, you have no need to think about these sharks, correct?

Wrong. If this is the case, you should *be* one of the sharks. The natural direction of business is always growth, and if you're not taking advantage of high-value opportunities to expand a well-run operation, you're missing the chance to strengthen the business community as a whole, while rewarding yourself in the process.

The business owners who can't get these things right are ultimately doing no favors for their employees, their customers, or even themselves.

If you are one of these business owners who are not getting it right, you're probably better off taking a shark's offer than continuing to struggle. And the shark can probably shore up your business in a way that you can't – because if you could, you would have already done so.

Sharks are not shy about hunting for their prey. So, if you are struggling, you'd better start doing it right. You know how sharks get when they smell blood.

Wake-Up Call: Vince Lombardi started training camp with these words, "Gentlemen, this is a football." Today I want to start your wake-up call with, "Readers, this is a balance sheet."

35

GROW OR DIE: THE MOST ABUSED
PHRASE IN BUSINESS

———

I have mixed emotions about the phrase "grow or die" in business. On the one hand, it's great advice, and I agree with it 100 percent.

However, the problem I have with it is not so much the literal words. It's the way people usually apply it, which typically doesn't lead to the kind of growth companies need to thrive — or to avoid dying.

In fact, "grow or die" is one of the most abused terms in business. A lot of that has to do with the nature of entrepreneurs, who are often more inclined to go-go-go than they are to think about where they're going.

So, when you tell a go-go-go entrepreneur to "grow or die," it begs the question: What does it mean to grow? Too often that entrepreneur will simply assume growth refers to one thing and one thing only — and that's top-line revenue.

Now I'm all about bringing in more revenue. However, it's a mistake to think that's the only form of growth your company needs. It's also a big mistake to think you can become more successful by focusing only on revenue growth and not on the things that typically lead to it.

Growth done right means becoming better in a lot of ways. It means improving in employee engagement. It means enhancing the value you offer your customers. It means conceiving and perfecting products that truly serve a need in the market. It means building a company culture that emphasizes excellence in every aspect of operations. Chiefly, it means growing profitability first.

Absent this focus on profitability, products, and culture, revenue can become little more than vanity for the owner. Your top line may look good, but if you haven't grown in these other areas, you're not in the strongest position to parlay that higher revenue into real, sustained success.

I can tell you firsthand I won a lot of trophies and got a lot of recognition for revenue growth, but I would give them all back to have had more profitability. There will always be people willing to help you grow your revenue by buying your under-priced product or service. Find a way to grow your business with the right buyers, at the right price, and at the right profitability.

The entrepreneur who's chasing only after higher revenues will tend to put outsized emphasis on sales. He is sure the product or service is great, and that he has exactly the right people, and that all the company needs is more people buying.

This is the entrepreneur who doesn't think there's any definition of growth apart from simply taking in more money. Everything else? He's sure he's got that mastered.

In fact, the great companies have often had seasons of growth in which they elevated themselves in different areas. This was true of Apple, where they spent time focusing on employee engagement, then more time focusing on client value. All along the way they kept zeroing in on what they needed to accomplish to become a truly great company.

Many entrepreneurs are relatively young. They're full of energy and they have great ideas, but they're lacking in experience and education, so they may not understand everything that's required to achieve what you can call a growing company.

Although there are many areas of growth you should focus on, here are three that make a huge difference:

1. Better products.
2. Better people to deliver the products.
3. Better sales and marketing.

Beyond that, you can add better financial management, better deployment of resources, and better improvement processes. These are all things that lead to more revenue, so they're all part of growth.

If I had to name one thing that would define your priority in growth, it wouldn't be revenue. It would be the value you represent to your customers. Grow in that area, and just about everything else will take care of itself. Of course, to achieve that, you have to grow in all the areas mentioned above — and that will likely require various stages of growth to get you to the goal.

Skipping all this and just focusing on sales gets it exactly backward. When you're truly excellent in all the areas I've described here, the company's offering practically sells itself. I'm not saying you don't need to get out there and market it, but it's not hard to make the sale when the value is that clear. People will always buy what gives them more value and helps them to achieve their goals.

If this is what you mean by growth, then I agree with grow or die. Failing to grow in all these ways will leave you in your competitors' dust, because they will surpass you. Grow or die is a great term as long as you understand there are stages to business growth, and as long as you're committed to what those stages will require of you.

When grow or die just means "bring in more revenue," someone needs to sit down and have a serious talk with the entrepreneur who's pushing that thinking. That's not growth at all. It's an ill-fated attempt to get more people to throw money at you when you haven't done the things that would allow you to say you've earned it.

By the way, the ultimate prize for all this isn't more revenue. It's more profit. If you want a monetary measure of your business's success, that's it. Lots of companies bring in revenue but don't make much profit, because they haven't grown in the areas we've discussed here. Do the hard work, and accomplish the real growth, and then your profit will prove to be a much more satisfying one.

Wake-Up Call: Grow profit or die.

36

THE INTERNET CAFÉ: A LESSON IN TIME MANAGEMENT AND LEAD PRE-QUALIFICATION

E veryone wants to put his or her best foot forward for a new business opportunity, and I'm certainly not going to criticize anyone for going all out to win an account.

However, you do learn a lot from your experiences, and one of my earliest attempts to win a big piece of business taught me a lot about preparing for — and prequalifying — prospects.

I'm going all the way back to the mid-1990s here, and that's important because you might recall that the internet back then was a very new thing. It wasn't common to have access to it in your home, and most people had to get online either at work or at a library.

At the time, I was involved with a business selling a machine that printed credit cards, membership cards, and similar products. A referral source turned me on to an opportunity with a burgeoning internet café, whose prospective founder wanted to offer membership cards to his patrons.

It was right up our alley. This was just the kind of business we had in mind when we took this machine to the market. I saw it as an excellent opportunity and was determined to go in and make an excellent presentation.

That meant actually packing up one of the machines, and a variety of other presentation materials, and heading to downtown Grand Rapids, where I'd be meeting with two father-and-son business partners.

Parking is not easy downtown — even if you're not hauling a credit card printing machine — but you do what you have to do to get a piece of business, right? I entered the conference room confidently and greeted the four men. I had my presentation all ready. I just needed to wait for the right moment to get it started. That's when I started to realize nothing about this meeting was going to go the way I expected.

One of the father-son combinations consisted of the would-be internet café owner and his dad, whose money the son needed to start the business. I was under the impression the venture was already going forward, and my only challenge was to convince them my machine was exactly what they needed.

As it turned out, the father and son were not on the same page at all. The son was gung-ho. He was convinced the internet was going to be the next big thing and that it would change everything. He couldn't imagine a better business idea than an internet café because internet access was at a premium.

On the surface, you could see his point. Anyone who remembers getting floppy disks in the mail from AOL, or paying per minute for dialup connections, can relate to the appeal of having a place to go where you could get on the internet much more easily. (Granted, there wasn't as much to see as there is now, but it seemed pretty exciting at the time.)

The father had a different perspective, and it wasn't an old fuddy-duddy one, either. He was completely convinced of the internet's staying power. His question concerned the viability of the internet café. The father wasn't so sure that internet access would always be at such a premium. He believed it was entirely possible that the day would come when people could get online access much more easily

—possibly even in their own homes, and without having to tie up a phone line or deal with slow speeds and high per-minute access rates.

If that happened (and of course it did) the internet café would become an obsolete concept very quickly. For that reason, his son's enthusiasm notwithstanding, the father was not prepared to invest in the business.

For more than 30 minutes I sat there awkwardly, watching the two of them debate this issue. The longer it went on, the clearer it became that it would be fruitless to present my machine to them since it was far from certain this internet café would ever open, and it never did.

So, what did I do wrong? No one could have foreseen the uncomfortable father and son dynamic that ended up dominating the meeting. However, I could have done a better job of pre-qualifying the opportunity.

I could and should have asked more questions on the phone before I ever showed up for the meeting. Questions like:

Do you have a definite launch date for the business?

Do you have your financing in place?

Do you have a budget for equipment like mine?

Have you committed to patron memberships that would necessitate printing the cards?

These are not unreasonable or intrusive questions. None of them involve amounts of money, nor do they ask who is providing the financing. They simply would have given me a sense of how viable the opportunity was. I might have concluded from the answers that I'd be better off waiting to make an in-person presentation when the owners were more committed to going forward.

In the end, it only cost me time. However, you only have so much time, and you can't afford to be constantly wasting it on situations that seem to be good opportunities but aren't.

More than 20 years in business has taught me a lot about the questions to ask and the signs to look for. I still go all-out for new business opportunities that are solid and imminent. You should too. While I don't sell those machines anymore, I absolutely bring my best whenever I have a chance to present to a business that's ready for my services.

However, I absolutely prequalify every situation before I go through all that. That improves my closing rate significantly. Even more, it saves me a lot of time I could be using more productively than sitting in front of a father and son who don't see eye to eye.

That internet café never did open, and internet cafés weren't a thing for long, for all the reasons that father suspected. Eventually, someone else bought that machine, and I trust they put it to good use. Just like I've learned to do with my time.

Wake-Up Call: You aren't prequalifying leads, and it's wasting your time.

37

ASK THE HARDEST QUESTION EVER IN SALES

———

I t's hard to approach a client and ask the tough questions. But as salespeople, we have been taught to ask questions that stretch us, such as:

What do you want?

What is your budget?

What is it going to take for my company to win this bid?

May I meet with the decision maker?

However, the hardest question to ask is: Why didn't we win, or why didn't we get the deal?

The failure to ask, "Why didn't we win?" is killing companies because this is the most important question to ask. When you don't win the account, do you ask the company: "Why did we lose? What could we have done differently? What would it have taken to win?"

It's really a human problem because no one wants to know the truth. It's akin to the fact that no one wants to know why his or her baby is ugly. It's like asking, "Why is my baby ugly?"

The failure to ask the question is stopping you from learning or getting better. You don't necessarily learn from your wins. You learn from your losses, especially when it comes to sales.

When you ask, "Why didn't I win?" you get incredible data that you can't get anywhere else.

Why don't we ask this question? The first reason is that no one wants to know. If we find out what's wrong, we'll probably have to go do something about it. Or, it could be something that we can't change. In some cases, you'll find out the reason for why you lost, and you'll be happy that you lost.

Sometimes the reason you lost is because it's something that you can't do. IKEA is a great example of this. They lose deals every day, and they are okay with that. They are not going to change who they are to make you happy. They specialize in furniture that is not assembled, and that is flat packed. It costs a lot to ship wasted space. Customers may not like this about IKEA's model, but IKEA is not going to change. Apple is the same way. They lose a lot of customers because their products are part of a closed system. You can only purchase apps for your Apple phone from the Apple App Store.

Another reason we don't ask is that we've already been rejected, and we don't want to be rejected for a second time. Most people say, "They've already said that they don't want to do business with me. I don't want to ask a second time and be rejected again." It's like asking a girl to prom, and she tells you no. Then you ask, "Why not?"

We see it as a waste of time to spend more time on this type of account. After all, we didn't win. Let's just move on and go to the next thing. I can see the logic in that, but the challenge is that you're missing a great learning opportunity.

I don't always ask this question, but as a senior leader in business, this is one of the most important things I have had to learn to do after I didn't win a deal. I have to ask, "Why didn't I win? What could I have done better?"

I remember the time I didn't live this principle out. It was about two years ago. I had the opportunity to present my proposal to a company to provide Scaling Up coaching for a year. I had developed an annual contract for this prospect who was out of town, a long six-hour drive from my home. After a grueling drive, I botched the presentation. I knew I could have done much better. I knew I wouldn't get the deal because I fumbled my presentation.

During my long car ride home, I evaluated my poor presentation and all the hard work my team had pored into winning this account. A couple of weeks later, the prospect called and said, "We went with another coach." I was so disappointed in my performance that I forgot to ask why I didn't get the account. I assumed it was the presentation, but it was probably something bigger, such as what I was offering or the cost.

I missed an opportunity because I blamed a presentation. I look back with regret at missed opportunities too. Don't let anything stop you from asking that question.

After this fumbled proposal, I came up with some tricks to make it easier to ask the question. The first one is the easiest one, and it's the trick I rely on. During the sales process, especially if it's a lengthy process that involves a lot of work on my part, I ask the client for permission to ask the question later. I say, "If I do all of this and I don't win, would you be willing to share with me why you went with another option? I also want you to tell me how I could improve."

Set expectations up front that you are going to ask and gain commitment that they will tell you, because this is the easiest way to get it done.

If you forget to do that beforehand, ask the question later by appealing to the universal desire to get better. Call them and say, "Thank you for your time. I have one last request. I'm trying to get better. How I get better is by understanding why my company didn't win. Would you be willing to review that with me?" Everyone wants to get better, and most humans want to help others improve.

One final shortcut is to blame it on your boss. Just get on the phone and say, "I hate to bother you. I feel awful even asking this, but one of the things my boss makes me do is put down why we lost a deal. I can't make something up because he'll know if I did. So, can I get a genuine answer from you in case he ever checks?"

The hardest question to ask is, "Why didn't I win this account?"

However, it's also the most important one. You have to implement this into your sales process today. After you lose — or even after you win — ask why. The answers may surprise you, but they will give you the data you need to get better.

Wake-Up Call: You are being rejected every day. You don't know why, and that's hurting you.

38

BEING PARALYZED BY POOR GROSS PROFITS

———

Being paralyzed by poor gross profit is like sleep paralysis. It's absolutely horrible! A lot of business owners get paralyzed by poor gross profit. Have you ever felt that way? It's like when you wake up from a dream and you can't move. Your body is still secreting those neurotransmitters, GABA, and glycine.[1] You can wake up and be frozen for a few seconds. If you've ever experienced it, for most people it's a terrifying few moments. You've just woken up, and you can't move, but you don't know why.

Having very low gross profits in a very competitive, hard-to-advance market, is the same feeling as sleep paralysis. When you're in bed, you eventually start moving, but the cycle with low gross profits keeps repeating itself.

One of the most frustrating and distressing things as an advisor is to go into a company with low gross profits and help them. We always hear about tight, competitive markets, where there isn't a lot of gross profit. People say, "Oh, I've got to make this up on volume. I've got to figure this out." When I hear this, I just clench up and my heart breaks for the person. I get so frustrated for them.

If you can't find adequate gross profit, it's like nearly drowning, yet still clinging to life. You can never really grow the business because you don't have the resources to grow. However, you never go out of business because there are plenty of people willing to buy your product at a low gross profit. If you sell at low gross profit, you'll always have a ton of customers. After all, who doesn't want a great deal? If you're selling to consumers or other businesses and your gross profit isn't appropriately aligned, you'll always be in this plateau where you can't seem to grow. With a low gross profit, people can't seem to break free from the cycle.

Why am I talking about low gross profits and discouraging you? I'm going to tell you something that is easy for me to say, but hard for you to do. You need to solve the root cause of your low gross profit issue. I bet, right now as you're reading this, you're thinking, "Wade, I'm in a low gross profit business. How am I going to change that?"

If you don't figure out how to solve the root cause of your low gross profit, you'll always be trapped. Here are some ideas about how to get out of it. First, you won't excel by doing the very same things that others do better than you. You excel by doing something different than everyone else. I'm going to bring up some examples. One is Starbucks and the other is IT Cosmetics.

Starbucks started selling coffee at an extremely high price when you could buy coffee at a gas station for a lot lower price. Good friends of mine, Jamie and Paulo Lima, founded IT Cosmetics. Their company was founded by mere mortals — just like you and me. When they started IT Cosmetics, other cosmetics had been dominating the industry for years. However, they found out how to be competitive in that business and how to make money. They sold IT Cosmetics to L'Oréal in 2016 for $1.2 billion.[2] They succeeded by doing something different. You can't do everything the same as other companies and get better gross profits.

Second, if you are in a low profit margin, you have to go where the margin pools are. What do I mean by margin pools? In every industry, there is a 7-10 percent margin pool. There are people who are willing to spend more for something, such as better quality or better customer service. If you can find that group of people willing to spend extra money, you move out of that very competitive space into a highly profitable space. Every industry has that. Clothing companies, like Gucci and Gap, are doing well even though the industry is competitive. These companies are going out and chasing profit pools. The reality is that there's not a bad industry. Your industry with low profit margins isn't bad; you're just chasing the wrong area.

Third, you have to force yourself to move — to stop being paralyzed — and take a risk. Tell everyone in your company, "We have found something that will make a difference." Maybe you tell them, "We are going to invest in a new piece of equipment, or we are going into a new market." You need to find that one domino that will knock all the other dominoes over. For example, Go Daddy took a big risk on a Super Bowl ad, and it made a huge impact on their business. I'm not saying you should risk it all, but you need to take some risks.

If you have good gross profits, there will come a time when your gross profits become eroded. Competitors will see what you are doing and come into the market, and eventually gross profits will erode. Every year, you have to look at what you can do to be different. Ask yourself, "What are the profit pools I should be chasing?" (They could be changing.)

> **Pro Tip:** If you do have good gross profit and extra money, take two or three of your smartest people and put them in an office across town for three to six months. Tell them, "Figure out how to put me out of business. Find something different that competitors could do to erode our gross profit. What are profit pools that you would go after as a competitor? What are the big risks you would take as a start up?"

Wake-Up Call: You have underperforming gross profit.

39

BELIEVE IN WHAT YOU'RE SELLING . . . OR ELSE

I f I tell you it's important to believe in your product before you try to sell it, you'll say, "Well, of course."

However, you'd be surprised how often people knowingly go down the path of offering a product or service without even thinking about whether they embrace its value. I often hear entrepreneurs say, "I don't care what business I'm in as long as I can build a great company and provide jobs for people."

Maybe it's not that difficult to understand that mindset. After all, when you're selling product lines in 35 different categories, surely the CEO hasn't personally tried and fallen in love with all of them.

And hey, even if you don't personally believe in the value of the product, someone will! Maybe all you have to do is come up with enough convincing selling points and repeat them often enough, and your own personal belief will be irrelevant. All of that is tempting to believe, but let me tell you, it will not work.

For one thing, as an entrepreneur, you are usually the primary salesperson — at least at the outset. The reason people like working with entrepreneurs is that they get the opportunity to deal directly with the visionary. But who wants to deal with a visionary who doesn't buy or believe in his or her own vision?

People are more insightful than they are sometimes given credit for, and buyers can spot a person who's trying to sell a proposition they're not authentically interested in — or wouldn't buy themselves.

Think about the way sales meetings often progress. The person trying to make the sale might start with a set of talking points, and maybe the talking points are convincing on a certain level. However, most people don't buy on the strength of the talking points alone. The talking points just get the discussion rolling, followed by an in-depth discussion of the product or service under consideration.

If you're a discerning customer, you will want to know a lot about how this product or service will make you more successful. The entrepreneur who believes in what's being sold can have this conversation with you all day long and will do so with enthusiasm. The one who's just trying to convince you will revert back to the same talking points and will sometimes seem defensive.

People aren't stupid. They can spot this. Consumers don't buy the way they used to — just seeing a clever ad or an attention-grabbing sign and responding to it. They expect real engagement and interaction. Someone who's trying to fake it will be easily exposed.

If the entrepreneur can't exude that confidence in the product, how do you expect it to be embraced by salespeople if and when the company ever grows? When you train salespeople to sell your product, one of the most important elements of that training is to make sure they know the value proposition: Why will the customer be better off if they buy this?

I remember sitting in a presentation rehearsal one time, and it was clear the CEO wasn't confident about how the presentation was going to go. In his frustration, he threw up his hands and declared, "We're gonna have to do a lot of dancing to sell this."

Imagine the message that sent to the other members of the team. Essentially, they had just been told by the boss that the product wouldn't benefit the client. Under the circumstances, how could they be expected to convince the client it would be a benefit to buy? (Spoiler: The client didn't buy. Shocking, I know.)

If you're going to get your salespeople selling effectively, then you have to ooze genuine confidence in the value of the product or service when you're training them. You can't do that if you don't believe in the value of it yourself.

So, there are some clear imperatives here for entrepreneurs. First, if you're thinking about going into a line of business you don't believe in, don't. I don't care what your market research shows you. If you wouldn't buy it, you're not going to be able to sell it.

I am not saying you shouldn't start a business. I am not saying your company shouldn't branch out into new products and services. I am saying this: If you're not sold on the idea, then improve it and innovate it until you do believe in it. If you can't get there, then you might have to scrap it entirely and come up with something different. Improve it, innovate it, or scrap it if you're not buying your own value proposition. It's better than realizing you've made a mistake once you've invested all kinds of time and money into the new product or service.

But what if it's too late? What if you're already operating your company, and you realize you're struggling precisely because you don't believe in the value or service of your core product? This is when the imperative to innovate is greater than ever. You have to look objectively at what you're selling and decide why it doesn't work for you. Then you have to determine what would represent real value, and innovate to whatever extent is necessary to improve the product or service, to the point where it passes your value test.

Granted, there are some people who have convinced themselves they believe in their product or service because they want so badly to believe it. They don't, though, and they'll realize it at the worst possible moment.

For now, let's just make sure you don't go down this road and find yourself having to clean it up later. Take the time to produce a quality product or service so you can sell something that you believe in.

Wake-Up Call: If you don't believe in the product or service you sell, no one else will.

40

BAG THE BONUS: THERE ARE BETTER WAYS TO COMPENSATE YOUR TEAM

M any of the companies I advise are looking for the best way possible to structure their compensation. They know there's a correlation between achievement and reward, and they want to find the structure that leads to the most company success and the best outcomes possible for team members.

Those are the right goals, so let me start with the first step necessary to achieve those goals: Get rid of bonuses.

I'm not saying no one should receive anything beyond their salary or wage. In fact, I'm saying the opposite of that, as you'll soon see. However, the bonus is the least effective and least logical way of doing it.

In most people's minds, the bonus is essentially a gift. They often associate it with Christmas. When they receive it, it feels like a gigantic act of benevolence on the part of their employer – maybe something that will pay for that year's gifts or a special holiday trip.

I can understand why employees would like to receive a bonus. As a business strategy, giving out bonuses doesn't make any sense for a simple reason: They're not tied to anything the employee accomplished.

There are two better ways to do this. They are similar, but they have important distinctions. One is incentive pay. The other is at-risk pay.

Incentive pay is more familiar to most people, so let's start with that. It's basically the idea that you can earn something over and above your salary or wage by accomplishing certain things. I'm convinced that every employee should have the opportunity to earn some sort of incentive that's tied to the employee's performance.

It should not be based on time worked because time isn't necessarily achievement. Also, it should not be based on overall company performance because that could rob a high-achieving individual of the incentive to do well.

An incentive-based pay structure should be based on something measurable the employee can achieve that's directly related to the company's own strategic goals. It should come in addition to the employee's salary or wage, and it should be structured in such a way that the company can always afford to pay the incentive, because it comes out of real rewards the employee's achievements earned for the company.

Granted, this is easier to do with some positions than it is with others. For a salesperson, structuring incentives is easy. You just give them a percentage of what they sell. It's harder to come up with metrics for a mail room employee, but that doesn't mean you can't do it. If you're paying someone to do anything for your company, you should have some sense of how the company benefits when they do that job well. So yes, a good performance in the mail room should accrue to the company's benefit in ways that can come back to that employee in the form of an incentive.

That also adds to the motivation of every employee to increase the value of what they do for the organization. It should even work for nonprofits and government entities because both have goals employees can work toward achieving. And they're easier to defend against public scrutiny than the payout of "bonuses," which might sound like sheer favoritism. If the extra compensation is based on incentive goals you can show were attained, that should end the criticism.

At-risk compensation is a little different, although it's roughly based on the same idea. In the at-risk model, there is a defined amount of compensation an employee can receive (whereas the incentive could theoretically be limitless if they achieve enough). Maybe the employee's total potential compensation is $100,000. But a portion of that – let's say $40,000 – is "at risk." The $60,000 is locked in (assuming no firings or anything of that nature), but the employee can only earn some or all of the additional $40,000 by reaching certain goals or performance measures.

An at-risk compensation arrangement has the benefit of focusing employees very intensely on the goals that matter most. It means there's a defined amount of money they are leaving on the table if they don't hit their goals.

A difference between the two is that incentives are usually a small percentage of an employee's compensation (although they could theoretically be larger for a very top performer), whereas the at-risk portion of compensation under the at-risk model is usually more significant.

You frequently see contracts like this in the National Football League. They're called "prove it" contracts, and they pay only a small base salary with the potential for more if the player hits certain goals in terms of games played and other performance measures depending on his position.

How much you'd want to put at risk is obviously a question to be worked out with the individual employee based on lots of variables. However, it protects the company against paying too much for an underperformer, while giving the employee every opportunity to earn the top of his or her potential pay package.

It also helps to answer a frequently asked question among employees: Why is this person paid more than that person? If the answer is based on measurable metrics, there should be no argument. The person who made less can get every opportunity in the following year to make more. They just have to perform.

Even the best compensation scheme won't matter if you don't hire the right people, put them in the right roles, and give them every opportunity to succeed at their jobs. You can't incentivize a bad worker into being a good one, but you can incentivize a good one to achieve optimal results.

By the same token, a company with a bad purpose or bad values can't escape the consequences of those problems by trying to incentivize people to do every little thing. For the right company with the right mission, structure and leadership, incentive-based and at- risk compensation structures are far superior to simply handing out bonuses. They give employees the chance to earn more, and to do so in a way that makes you more prosperous as well.

Wake-Up Call: Dump the bonus. Start using incentive pay.

41

HIRING A SALESPERSON? MAKE SURE YOU GET A HUNTER, NOT A FARMER

I f your company is ready and you decide to hire a salesperson, I want it to work out for you, which is why I'm giving you this warning. Don't make the mistake of thinking you're getting a hunter and ending up with a farmer.

The hunter is the salesperson who's going to go out there and create leads, no matter what it takes. The hunter will walk into a company's office and, with absolutely no hesitation, ask for a meeting with the CEO. The hunter will research prospects, reach out to lots of them, and do the work of turning a significant percentage of them into good leads.

When most people endeavor to hire a salesperson, this is what they envision — a bulldog who will be proactive and create opportunities. This is who you usually want.

Often, you think you're getting a hunter, but you end up with a farmer. The farmer may be very helpful at working the administrative side of sales. The farmer might upgrade your software and your record-keeping and might have interesting ideas about sales support material and various internal processes. If you have existing leads, the farmer will nurture them as best as he or she can.

What the farmer will not do well is generate leads. For many people, it is simply not their skill set, nor their personality, to aggressively seek out sales opportunities. That is definitely true of farmers. If you hire one thinking you're going to be showered with new leads, you'll quickly end up disappointed and wondering why this isn't working out as you had hoped.

Yet, this happens to a lot of companies. They become convinced during the interview process that they've got just the person they need, only to find out when the person settles into the job that it's not the case at all.

So how does this happen? Why is it so difficult for employers to tell the difference? One reason is that farmers, because they're knowledgeable about the sales process, tend to interview well. They know how to speak the language. They'll embrace your big goals and tell you they want to jump in and do everything they can to help you meet them. They can be convincing. However, your vision of what they'll do is not the same as theirs, and you'll discover that too late.

Another reason is that too many entrepreneurs, once they've fallen in love with the idea of hiring a salesperson, lose their objectivity. They want so badly to love whomever is in front of them that they don't think critically about what they're about to do. They want to make the hire and get on with it, and they don't want to send the professional-seeming person in front of them away while they keep on interviewing. That makes it easy for the farmer who knows how to talk like a hunter to get hired, and it happens far too often.

So let me tell you a bit about real hunters. If you want to hire one, you need to know a few things, starting with this: You might not even like them. A hunter will be aggressive with you. He or she will push you to make a decision right then and there, which might put you off, but that's what good salespeople do.

You won't see them taking a lot of notes. They won't be very detail oriented. They won't be focused on process. They might also be very emotional, with lots of ups and downs to their energy. They're also very attuned to the angles of people in the room, to the point where they'll seem to be engaged in psychological operations. You'll notice they address you a lot by your first name.

Things like this sometimes explain why the hunters don't get the job and the farmers do. The farmer will seem more professional, but all the things that bother you about the hunter are also what makes him or her effective. The hunter will knock the door down to get the opportunity you want him or her to create. The hunter doesn't worry about bothering people.

You've probably seen salespeople who prefer to email rather than call, because they're trying to be courteous and not catch people at a bad time. That seems professional, but it's not what gets results. The hunter will just pick up the phone and call and will work the lead aggressively.

The farmer will be more concerned with servicing the account once you've got it, which can appear to make sense. However, it is ultimately a distraction from what you want a salesperson to do, which is go out and create more leads. The hunter might also express an interest in servicing the accounts, but he or she won't put up as much of a fight on the issue, because there's more money to be made from new commissions.

Oh, by the way, the hunter will always push you to base as much compensation as possible on commission because the hunter is prepared to go out and take advantage of that system.

Spending $300 on an assessment will help you distinguish the hunter from the farmer. So will asking simple questions like, "Tell me how you generate new leads. (And how have you done it successfully in the past?)" But understand that the hunter is a different kind of person and might not appear to fit in well with your corporate culture.

That's fine. If the hunter is always in the office fitting in, then you haven't gotten yourself a hunter. You want the hunter out there knocking down other people's doors, because that's what you were expecting a salesperson to do in the first place, right?

If you are going to hire a salesperson, make sure you get a hunter.

It is better to wait for the right one than to fall in love too easily and find out you didn't get what you were expecting.

Wake-Up Call: You don't have enough new sales because you hired farmers, not hunters.

42

SQUELCH THE SEDUCTIVE DESIRE TO REDESIGN YOUR WEBSITE. INSTEAD, REDO YOUR FUNNEL.

I t's something I hear over and over again as I visit different companies: "Wade, we are so excited to be going through a website redesign, and it's going to make a big difference."

I always cringe whenever I hear that. It reminds me of other things in life where people haven't dealt with the root issue. Instead, they have dealt with the cosmetic side of it. For example, I've seen people have a leak in their roof and simply paint the wall that has been stained by water damage rather than repairing the roof. They've definitely dealt with the stain, but they haven't addressed the root issue. There are so many other examples, such as fighting with kids on the way to church and then smiling ear to ear when you get there as though nothing is wrong. I have done it; we've all done it.

In almost every case, the website wasn't the organization's problem. Whatever the real problem the company faced is still there; it hasn't changed.

There's a small caveat here. Websites do need to be updated regularly. They do get stale, so I'm not advocating for people to forget about a website redesign. However, a social media facelift, better

Google reviews, or an updated web presence won't fix the root problem in sales. Although these are good tools to use in a business, most companies are relying on these things for a cosmetic fix rather than addressing the root problem — the sales funnel issue.

What do I mean by a funnel issue? The sales funnel is a two-part process — the discovery of your product or service and the closing of the sale. People run into problems when they believe that a website redesign will drastically increase sales by creating more sales' opportunity. It won't, and this mistaken belief is their first problem. They need a good funnel process or funnel tools.

Here's why: Imagine sales as this big funnel, and you are trying to capture as many leads or buyers as possible to consume your service or product. Imagine that you're trying to get these leads or buyers to fall into your funnel. Businesses hope a new website will do that, and they miss the opportunity to focus on other things that will help leads fall into the funnel.

The second part of the problem is that companies need to develop or refine how they work their leads in the funnel. This process needs to be matured to move the leads to the bottom of the funnel, the part where you close.

In some ways, using the analogy of a funnel is one of the worst things we could do. In a funnel, as soon as you drop something in, it goes to the bottom. Gravity does all the work. However, in the real world, when we say, "Get things into your sales funnel," there is no gravity. Instead, forces are working in the other direction when it comes to your sales funnel. Leads are constantly being sucked out of your funnel — whether by competition, lack of money, or buyers not knowing if you are the right solution for them.

Whenever I hear talk about a website redesign, it's like a signal to me that we need to talk about the company's sales funnel.

Traditionally, what are the issues that need to be addressed with funnels? First, wanting to get more leads is a real need. As opposed to doing a website update, do an assessment of how you get leads into the funnel. For most companies, they are getting leads from sources they don't recognize. For example, companies often get leads from the owner's network, partnerships they have already created, and referrals. There are many things that bring leads into the funnel. Would you rather increase or optimize those things that are proven to work, or are you going after a website update, a social media campaign, or some new tool? It's not to say that's wrong, but it's just a small part of getting leads into that funnel.

I tell people, "You have to imagine that you have huge funnel, but a large part of it is covered up by cardboard. There is just a small hole in the funnel. Everything you do around marketing and lead generation will open the hole bigger and bigger and allow more leads to fall into the funnel."

However, some marketing tools open the funnel bigger than others. I want you to focus on the tools that will create the largest hole in your funnel. To do that, you need to have a robust discovery or debate to discover how you get your leads.

In most cases, companies are spending too much money on a small lead development tool, such as a website redesign, when most of that money could be redeployed to other marketing-driven activities that would have a better chance of bringing in leads. This website redo has become a default spending mechanism that makes us feel good. It triggers a feeling that makes us believe we will have better leads, but we don't.

Process

Once you find where the bulk of your leads come from, you have to identify that initial sales funnel process, which can be divided into two parts.

1. During the initial discovery, the clients find out if you meet their needs and if they like you and trust you. Do you check off the appropriate boxes for them? However, when customers go through the discovery process, many people fall out of the funnel. So, this is where the investment should be made. How do you make sure the leads that come in get the proper amount of attention and data to move them into second portion of funnel? Your website

will help with that discovery process, but it's not interactive enough. I encourage people to build the top part of that funnel to make it far more interactive.

2. The second part of the funnel is the closing process. You give them a proposal and answer questions. This second portion has a higher success rate because clients do a lot of research before asking for a proposal. This "closing process" should be well documented, and just about anyone in your company should know how to do it. If this is true, you should be able to achieve a 50% close ratio once a client or prospect asks for a proposal. By the way, a prospect or client should always ask for a proposal. Read that again, they should always ask. You should not have to push it on them. If you have to push your proposal by saying, "Would you like us to give you a proposal?", you haven't really sold them. The first part of your funnel is only working well when the clients get to the closing point and ask to see a proposal.

With a proposal in hand, if you are not closing 50% of deals, you have some serious work to do in your closing portion of the process. It could be the proposal, your product, or your people, but most likely it's your lack of prepared and practiced handling of your client's objections. You should have an answer for the most common objections that clients have.

Assuming your closing is 50%, shift your focus back to discovering the best way to get leads into the funnel and open the top up. Be purposeful about answering that question: Where do the bulk of our leads come from? Don't just say, "We are going to redo our website." The second thing is to redeploy that capital in the first part of the funnel. Automate and streamline the top part of your funnel. That's where you're losing sales. You're not losing sales in the bottom part of the funnel.

Many times, people do all their decision making prior to ever talking to you. That's where the investment needs to be made.

Remember, build that top part of the funnel, and make it more interactive. You need a great website, but your funnel is the real key to improving sales.

Pro Tip:

1. Improve your ability to get leads into the funnel with unique tools and sales discovery.
2. Create a top of the funnel process that guides your client through the discovery process and ensures you are there every step of the way. Do this by first mapping out your "buyer's journey."
3. There is only one best way to sell or close your product or service. Discover that, document it, teach it, and practice it. You should be able to close 50% of all proposals.

Wake-Up Call: Your funnel is only working at half strength, and you are only getting half the sales you should be.

PART V

LEADERSHIP

43

NO ONE ACHIEVES PEAK PERFORMANCE WITHOUT A COACH

I love the adrenaline rush and the personal sense of satisfaction that come from coaching a person or team to victory, and I always have. The word coach can often veer toward a sports theme in most people's heads; however, for me, coaching is more than just a sports-based activity. Today, we call my job — what I love to do — mentoring. And while that may be more appropriate, I still love the word coach.

Growing up, I always enjoyed working with kids younger than me, showing them the short cuts. As I got older, that impulse continued into high school and in my dorm, where I saw myself as a coach to many of the younger students. I started to grasp my love for coaching during our end-of-year basketball game of seniors versus the rest of the team. This had become a yearly tradition, and that year we had a very strong senior class. On the evening of the game, sensing the fact that the seniors had an advantage, our coach took an active role in coaching underclassmen against the seniors. At the time, if you had asked me if I wanted to sit on the sidelines or play, the answer would have been easy: PLAY.

Unfortunately, I didn't get a lot of time on the court based on my skill level compared to the other seniors. But that evening, that fact became my biggest asset and one of the pivotal points in my life. Near the end of the first quarter, the seniors were already down by 10. I clearly saw that without a good coach on the sidelines we would not win. I decided to take on the coaching role. I called a time-out, huddled up the seniors, and told them we needed a coach. I then told them I was going to do it. They all wanted the play time, so it was a no-brainer to let me coach and keep one more guy out of the rotation.

I could bore you with the details, but the bottom line is we went on to win that evening. It energized me to stand on the sidelines and direct the action. Even though I enjoyed the spotlight of playing, there is nothing like the feeling of coaching. You can't deny the high you get when you score or assist on a basket. Although for me, the feeling of coaching overcame that high easily. While many of my high school memories are not as clear as they once were, that night is still crystal clear. After we won, I felt better than I had felt after any other win. Our coach, who had taken the side of the underclassmen, came over and congratulated me for the win. After that day, I knew I wanted to coach and build teams.

Since then, I have not had a chance to do any significant coaching in sports. I'm okay with that fact, because I have spent what seems like a lifetime coaching and mentoring individuals in business. I love the payoff of helping someone else advance in his or her job, beating a deadline, or finishing a big project. That pivotal moment in my life, when I discovered my "why" in coaching, changed the course of my professional career. I have endeavored (and will continue to endeavor) to be a mentor and coach in any role, and I'm convinced this has helped me succeed at a more rapid pace. The combination of being able to help others, and being open to being coached myself, has accelerated my career. Of course, I have many coaches and mentors to thank for helping me get this far.

We all get a chance to coach and mentor nearly every day. Looking for more success in your professional life? I want to encourage you to be more purposeful in your coaching. Mentoring is awesome, though I think a hybrid between coaching and mentoring is far better. It's just not enough to show someone how to do it; you have to encourage them through the process and help them find the answer. That night in 1992, when we came from behind to beat the underclassmen, I didn't show my fellow seniors how to win; I coached them to victory. They found a way to win.

If you are looking for great resources to help you get started coaching others, I would recommend *The Coaching Habit: Say Less, Ask More & Change the Way you Lead Forever* by Michael Bungay Stanier[1] and *Trillion Dollar Coach* by Eric Schmidt, Jonathan Rosenberg, and Alan Eagle[2]. These are great foundational books on coaching in business and life.

All this leads me to my life-long purpose of building teams. I have been fortunate to be an entrepreneur, which has given me a natural layup to my purpose in life. I have also been able to live this purpose as a father, friend, church member, and citizen. That night in 1992 set me on a lifelong path of building teams, and I have loved every moment. To all the teams I have been on over the years, I salute you!

Wake-Up Call: No one really wins without a coach. Winning is always easier with a great team!

44

HOW TO CONQUER HUMAN NATURE'S WAR AGAINST ACHIEVEMENT

Y ou've probably said it yourself – or something like it – in reference to a shortcoming, flaw or perceived weakness: "That's just me."

I'm sure you've heard other people do it too. They assign themselves to some sort of limitation, and instead of resolving to overcome it, they embrace it as part of their identity. They'll tell you they're not good at being punctual, or at following directions, or at patience, or at math. They're not expressing it as a self-improvement imperative. They're expressing it as a settled fact: "That's just who I am." Marshall Goldsmith highlighted this concept in his best-selling and must-read book *What Got You Here Won't Get You There.*[1] I love the concept, and think it deserves more exploration.

As leaders, we chafe at this idea of limitations because we want people to challenge themselves. We want people to seek improvement. We hope they will see their entire lives as journeys of growth, but the truth is that achievement and excellence are contrary to human nature.

There are so many examples of this. Consider the $900 car insurance payment an individual might need to make every six months. That doesn't sound so hard because all he has to do is put away $150 a month. But human nature is to put off saving, and the next thing he knows, he is at the six-month point and now he has to come up with $900. It's not that he didn't know the better way to do it. Human nature just led him not to do it that way.

Consider the person who struggles every day to be on time. She knows she needs to be at the office at 8:30 a.m., and she knows 90 minutes is not enough time to get ready and get there. The solution is to get up earlier than 7 a.m. That's obvious, but she keeps getting up at 7 a.m. Why? She does it because human nature tells her to resist the change and keep sleeping. It makes no sense to keep sleeping if her goal is to solve her punctuality problem.

Human nature always wars against excellence. So how can a leader combat this fact? Human nature is an awfully difficult enemy to fight. Do you have any hope of prevailing against it? You do, but it starts with achieving credibility, so your people will want to join you in the battle.

Before you can expect your people to work on changing their human nature, they are going to watch and see what you do with yours. I know I have my own issues, like being on time. I also struggle with overestimating my ability to remember things. Sometimes I procrastinate (but I'll deal with that later).

If I expect my people to deal with their own human-nature issues, I have to own mine. That doesn't mean I need to be vomiting my problems before my people. They don't need that, and it doesn't accomplish anything. However, I need to be willing to admit my problems and demonstrate that I'm taking steps to correct them.

If I know I struggle to be on time, I have to develop new habits that will get me places earlier – and be upfront about how it works and how I'm following it. If I know I procrastinate, I need to show my people I'm moving things from the back burner to the front. I need to let them see that I'm getting things done as promised. If I know I struggle to remember things, I need to be upfront about embracing a new system in which I write things down and log them somehow. And I need to rely on that system and let the results speak for themselves.

Once my people see that I've done these things, they will recognize that improvement and growth are priorities for our company, and they will be more willing to embrace the same imperatives for themselves.

This is the only way to battle that excessive need to be me. You've seen this in action many times, I'm sure. It's the person who announces his or her limitations with defiant pride, saying, "I'm just not good at that," or "I'm just not gifted for that."

The truth, of course, is that many of the things you claim to be "just not gifted at" are not gifts at all. You don't need to be gifted to be on time. You don't need to be gifted to write down appointments. You just have to decide to do it, and then put in the work to identify what's necessary for you to do it consistently and successfully.

Yes, much of that work goes against your human nature, but that doesn't mean you can't do it. It just means you have to make decisions that are contrary to your inclinations. It means you have to decide you value achievement more than you value what's comfortable and familiar.

Anyone can do this. They just have to decide to.

Leading by example is one of the most familiar terms in the lexicon of business, but it's rarely more important than it is here. People don't always like who they are, but they get comfortable with who they are, and they learn to abide in that state. They may want to be better, but they're not always sure they can handle what it will take. So they default to just "being me" for lack of a compelling reason to do otherwise.

You have to show them the imperative is great, and the rewards are worth the effort and the risk. Human nature *will* hold you back from achievement, but only if you've made the decision that it's going to master you. Before your employees take steps to free themselves from that mastery, they're going to need to see you do it first.

. . .

Wake-Up Call: The only way to get your team to fight their human nature is to start changing yours.

45

NO, DON'T SET EXPECTATIONS FOR YOUR EMPLOYEES WITHOUT ENGAGING THEM FIRST

J ust about everyone has a term for how you measure performance. Some call it metrics. Some call it key performance indicators. You probably have a term of your own.

I am not all that concerned about the term you use. I'm more concerned with how you determine what's expected of your people. Or, more to the point, who is involved with that decision-making.

The easy thing to do, especially if you're focused on showing everyone you're in charge, is to simply dictate the expectations and let everyone know they're expected to meet them. Many a boss has gone down this road, thinking clarity is all that's needed to get performance out of people.

Dictating expectations is not how you get the best results. If you do, people will give you the minimum effort required to deliver on those expectations, and they will give you no more than that. This is human nature. With no say in the expectations you set, your employees won't buy-in or give their best effort to deliver optimal results.

So how do you get that? I am certainly not suggesting that everything be done by consensus. Someone has to be the decision maker, and sometimes it is necessary to apply the knowledge you have as a leader and assert that certain things are nonnegotiable.

However, that doesn't exclude engaging your people in a process to help define expectations. As the leader, it is your job to define the goals that must be achieved. Effective leaders understand that goals are best achieved by teams who have input on the measures that will get them there.

My observations from 20-plus years in the business world tell me that the best results come from teams who have been asked by the boss:

How can we work together to accomplish these goals?

How will we measure, daily or weekly, the process to get there?

What does the team need from each team member in order to get there?

People appreciate having input on these issues, but it's more than that. Getting your team's input will help you align your expectations with their strengths, their thinking, and their understanding of how the team is structured.

You know a lot about your team, but you don't know everything. Hearing from the members of your team about how best to accomplish these goals will allow you to set expectations they are more likely to master on an ongoing basis.

Consider the business goals of a baseball team. The owner of the team wants as many people as possible buying tickets, gear, and food. That's how he makes money.

One crucial element of any strategy to achieve this will involve winning games. The more games you win, the better the chance people will buy tickets, gear, and so forth. But you don't want your starting pitcher looking around in the stands and thinking to himself, "We only drew 15,000 tonight. I should do something about this."

No, his job is to pitch well. This might be obvious when we're talking about baseball. However, within your company, how many people are thinking about too many things they shouldn't be? If you asked them what the expectations should be for them to meet the larger goal, what might they tell you that would help keep them focused on the right things?

Simply asking the question will boost the contribution each employee makes to achieving the larger goals.

Also, you will boost engagement — a lot. It will give you a solid helping of what Gallup calls discretionary effort.[1]

What is that discretionary effort? Let's go back to our statement earlier about how employees who have expectations dictated to them will give you the minimal effort required to meet those expectations. The minimal effort involves no discretionary effort. Discretionary effort is what they're willing to give you beyond mandated requirements because they want to.

Gallup's research shows that engaged employees give more discretionary effort.[2] It doesn't necessarily mean they're working harder. It means they're more engaged and invested in achieving the expectations that have been set — because they helped to set them. Plus, they had the chance to tell you what they do well.

Let's use another baseball example. What if a pitcher had the capacity to throw 20 pitches each game? That's not a lot if you know baseball. It will barely get you through one inning. But what if he's absolutely amazing throwing those 20 pitches? Is there a role for him? Absolutely. That's called a closer, because you can use him in the ninth inning when the pressure is on to protect a lead and close out a game.

However, if you try to use him as a starting pitcher, he'll start getting knocked around by the second or third inning. Letting him tell you what you should expect from him allows you to define a role in which he can thrive and offer the maximum contribution.

Why not do the same with your team members? It's still up to you to define the goals, and it's still up to you to set the parameters in which your expectations of them have to fit. I do not believe in 100 percent management by consensus.

However, you do need to listen to them and take advantage of the information they give you when setting expectations. This is how you'll get the most engaged, the best aligned, and the most effective workforce. In other words, the best results.

Start working with your team to set expectations. When you set expectations, you risk your team not performing to their full potential.

Wake-Up Call: If you set the expectations without input, you will receive substandard performance from your team.

46

WHAT TO DO ABOUT BAD LEADERSHIP TEAMS

———

M arcus Buckingham and Ashley Goodall released a wonderful book in 2019 called *Nine Lies About Work*.[1] It debunks a lot of long-held concepts about the professional world. One of them is the idea that culture drives employee engagement and satisfaction. In fact, the book asserts, teams actually drive company culture, and that's what drives employee satisfaction.

I was thinking about the role of leadership teams in driving company culture and satisfaction. Usually if you're struggling to grow, or to scale, or to have success in any other way you would define it, you can trace that struggle in some way to your leadership team.

Patrick Lencioni has said that trust is the most important characteristic for a good leadership team, so it's no surprise that a leadership team would function poorly if it's populated by toxic people who don't trust each other.[2]

If you want to avoid the problem of a bad leadership team, there are four important principles that you need to consider:

1. Limit the size of the team. This is often difficult because there are so many company executives who seem to belong. You think to yourself that you've got to have your CFO, you've got to have marketing, and sales, and IT, and legal, and HR . . . and soon you've got a leadership team of 12 to 15 people. Big mistake. Keep the leadership team to eight. Beyond that, it becomes very difficult for the leadership team to function well. There are too many voices at the table and too many relationships. It's hard to tell some people they're not going to be on the leadership team, but it's necessary if you want the team to function efficiently.

2. Make it clear that membership on the leadership team isn't permanent for anyone but the leader. (This also helps when limiting the size of the team). Since membership isn't permanent, people understand that if they're told they're not on the team this year, it's not some sort of insult or point of disrespect. Maybe this year the CFO isn't included because the IT manager needs to be. Establishing this principle will help you manage group dynamics.

3. Make sure the team has very well-run meetings, and I'm talking about the mature meetings that Lencioni talks about in his numerous leadership books, such as *Death by Meeting*[3] and *The Five Dysfunctions of a Team*[4]. It's not enough that people just get together and talk about whatever they want. The meetings should be focused and designed to accomplish important tasks.

4. Manage the relationships on the leadership team. Everyone doesn't have to be best friends, but you have to make sure the team is healthy and well-aligned. You have to keep an eye out for undercurrents and challenges. If you don't, bad actors can remain on the team and poison it.

These are good rules to follow in forming and running a good team, but let's say you already have a bad one. How do you fix it?

There are some important things to remember. First, be careful of the speed at which you change out people on the team. The best plan is to make only one change every six months. If you absolutely have to, you might be able to make two changes at a time. No more than that, or things become too destabilized. What if you have three bad members? Well, if you put three bad people on an eight-person leadership team, get rid of the two biggest problems, and maybe the third one won't be so bad when they're gone.

Second, when you're switching people out, be careful about who you add to replace them. Sometimes you can find someone who is too good for your company. (Yes, that is possible.) They might be a superstar executive from a big company, and you thought you had to go big with a hire to replace an underperformer. But make sure the new person actually fits in and works for the team you have.

Third, be intentional about team building. I'm not saying you have to take them for any of that "trust fall in the woods" type of team building, but there are great exercises you can do right in your office. I am a big fan of one called Lifeline, where you take your personal life, your business life, and your financial life and map out what's gone on for the past 40 years. It builds a lot of trust and teamwork.

Finally, here's a challenge for CEOs who can't stand their leadership teams and try to avoid meeting with them at all costs. Before you change the whole leadership team, consider: Is it you?

Often bad teams are associated with bad leadership. CEOs usually don't want to hear this, but maybe you have some significant work of your own to do in your life and in your journey. That's hard to hear, but the good news is that it's easier to work on yourself than to try to fix somebody else — and you have the power to do it.

Whatever you can do to fix your leadership team — whether it starts at the top or requires a whole team overhaul — it's essential to the success of any company. No organization can rise above its leaders.

· · ·

Wake-Up Call: Every Leadership team has at least one underperforming member. It's time to upgrade your team.

47

HOW DO AWARDS AND RECOGNITION DISTRACT YOU FROM WHAT REALLY MATTERS?

I t's human nature to enjoy being recognized for a job well done. No one is going to begrudge you that.

However, because it's human nature, the quest for acknowledgment can sometimes lead us down a path that seeks recognition instead of things that actually have more value. This is especially true in business.

We hear about these things all the time. This or that person got Employee of the Month. This or that company was named Supplier of the Year. And of course, everyone likes to describe themselves as "award-winning." Some of it is ego, but some of it can be useful in brand-building and marketing. I am certainly not saying there is no real value to awards and recognition.

However, I have personally fallen into the trap of pursuing awards and recognition in ways that actually ran counter to my larger strategic interests. More than 15 years ago, I owned a company that represented a major software manufacturer. In our first year working with them, I was very surprised to learn at their annual conference that we had won Supplier of the Year. I wasn't expecting it and didn't think much of it, but there it was, and it was a nice little feather in our cap.

The following year we lost to a competitor. Now that started to bother me. Having won it once, I didn't see why we shouldn't win it again. So, I got my team together and discussed strategies we could use to come back the third year and retake the award.

In order to be named this company's Supplier of the Year, it was important to sell a lot of this company's software. We were confident we could do that, and we put a lot of time, energy, and resources into the effort.

It worked! When year three came along, we were once again Supplier of the Year. We felt we had achieved something important professionally, and we felt a lot of satisfaction over it.

However, it came at a price. Looking back, I realize that selling this company's software — while it generated some welcome revenue — was not our most profitable line of business. We profited more from consulting services, and we would have been better off putting our efforts into building that part of the business.

However, the prospect of winning back this award was so enticing that we put disproportionate effort into making it happen. Not only that, but we were also offering discounts and deals that weren't in our best interests to improve our numbers selling this particular company's software products. In the end, we got the recognition, but we hadn't earned the profits we could have. And we hadn't positioned ourselves as strategically as we should have for the future of our business.

Yes, the recognition added a bit to our reputation. However, it didn't build our reputation as consultants, and I can't say the effort was worth the return.

A friend of mine experienced something similar around the same time. He had a client whose team was going gangbusters servicing a particular account. Since the account was structured in a pay-for-results sort of way, all their success was earning him a lot of money.

The team felt the account was going so well that they approached my friend and asked if they could spend some time submitting their work for a local industry award. They felt they had a shot at Best of Show. Although my friend isn't much of an awards guy, he didn't want to douse his team's enthusiasm, so he gave them the go-ahead.

They won Best of Show! It was pretty exciting. I remember him and his team going up to accept the award, and I could tell that he looked like he didn't know what he was supposed to do. It was a nice moment for all of them, and they got a nice shiny award that they took back to the office to put on display. Surely, they thought, it would be the first of many. However, less than two months later, they lost the account. Why? Because the client didn't see the value of the service the team provided, even though industry peers felt the work was award worthy.

He told me later that it taught him a huge lesson about awards. There's a difference between what your industry peers think is good work and what your client sees as bringing him or her value. As I know from my own experience, there's a difference between the work you do to get noticed and the work you do to set yourself up for long-term success.

The same is true with employees. Most companies believe it's smart to have some sort of employee recognition program, and they will often reward a job well done with gift certificates, spa days, lunches or whatever.

There's nothing wrong with this in theory, but are employers using these incentive programs as a substitute for the compensation that employees deserve? Think about it from an employee's perspective. Would you rather get a raise or a spa day? Remember, with the raise, you can pay for your own trip to the spa.

Of course, it's nice to have the recognition and to be praised in front of your peers. We all want that. It's human nature. But does it carry the value to match the gratification we feel from it?

Please, recognize your people and reward them. However, be sure the incentive is placed correctly. There are so many examples of staff going out of their way to win a pizza for lunch while missing a larger deal.

In the end, this is mostly about the entrepreneur, who is most likely to fall for the seduction of awards — just as I did many times in my 15 years as a CEO. In almost all cases, the value you gain from business maturity far exceeds the value of an award.

Wake-Up Call: Entrepreneurs chase recognition at the cost of profit. Avoid the seduction of awards, and enjoy the ones you had no idea you were winning.

48

MASTERING THE PATTERNS AND PLATEAUS OF GROWTH

G rowth is hard. You know that, of course, but have you ever defined what makes it hard?

I'm not talking about the daily work that's required to run your company, find customers, and keep your product or service excellent. That's hard enough.

In this case, I'm talking specifically about the changes that are required when we reach certain plateaus of growth. Of all the challenges growth presents, I believe the hardest is that growth doesn't allow us to remain what we are.

This is simply a matter of recognizing patterns. The best chess players usually succeed, not because they can necessarily anticipate an opponent's next move, but because they know how to recognize patterns in the game. Business is no different. There are patterns to business growth, and we can generally assign these patterns to certain plateaus where companies tend to get tripped up. Usually, these patterns become problems for business owners for one of three reasons: 1. They don't recognize the patterns. 2. They don't get the help they need to deal with them. 3. They don't accept the need to change.

At every distinguishable growth plateau, we can identify changes that plateau requires. From my experience, it's easier to reach these plateaus (with the exception of the last one) than it is to implement the changes they demand. Let's look at each one.

The First Plateau of Growth

The first plateau comes when you hit the $1 million mark and grow to between 5 and 10 employees.[1] Before this, you could probably rely on very informal management and communication systems. Maybe you weren't winging it or playing it fast and loose, but as long as you kept in touch with everyone on a regular basis, you probably had everyone in the loop and on board with the plan.

Once you've got 5-to-10 employees, you need more formal systems and processes. That's hard for a lot of entrepreneurs to accept, because they see the progress they've made doing it the old way. Plus, they figure they shouldn't fix what isn't broken. However, it's not that it's broken. It's that the business has reached another level, and the business needs greater sophistication to operate at that level.

The Second Plateau of Growth

The second plateau is when you hit $10 million in revenue, at which point you will have around 50 employees.[2] At this plateau, you've mastered the management and communication challenges you faced at the last plateau. You've got a management structure in place. You've started to realize you can't personally manage everything that happens on a day-to-day basis.

The challenge here involves financial discipline. For the first time, you will probably need a full-time CFO. You will need a relationship with your vendors and your bank that may involve managing a line of credit for the first time. And when you hit the $10 million mark in revenue, you will probably need an infusion of cash — whether that happens organically or someone from the outside injects cash into the business.

If you've saved money you've been earning along the way, that simplifies this challenge; there are a lot of entrepreneurs who lack the

188 | WADE W. WYANT

discipline to do that as they're growing. If you need an infusion of cash and you don't have it, you might have to give up some control of your business to get what you need to operate at this level. Otherwise, it's very difficult to bridge that growth gap.

Before this, you might have juggled your cash flow in creative ways — maybe borrowing from Peter to pay Paul. Maybe you found a way to use your vendors as a *de facto* bank. That won't work at this level.

You're also going to need better processes. You need better documentation and a way to make sure processes are followed. Good managers and leadership aren't enough to ensure this. You have too many people now, and without processes and procedures, there's no way you can keep all of them moving in the right direction.

The Third Plateau of Growth

The third plateau will find you between $50 million and $100 million in revenue.[3] At this level, it's crucial that you develop your next layer of leadership. As the entrepreneur, you're the founder and visionary. You're the idea person.

However, you probably need two or three layers of leadership between you and the front-line people who are delivering on the ideas. That's because teams can't work if they're too big. If you have 1,000 employees, they can't all function on a daily basis as one gigantic team. When was the last time you saw a baseball team with 1,000 players in the dugout? Good teams don't work that way because people get too far from leadership, and they can't identify their difference-making role.

A company with 1,000 employees needs to be broken down into smaller teams with individual leaders, and that's why your various levels of leadership are so important here.

Another challenge at this level is that you've suddenly hit people's radar. At $50 million or more in revenue, you've probably gotten some press, and maybe you've won some awards. People are starting to notice you. That's good, but it also means they're gunning for you. You've probably turned over a minimum of a hundred employees at this level. So, those folks have gone to other companies, and they've probably talked about you.

At each of the plateaus identified here, we've pointed to patterns you should be able to recognize and plan for as you grow. You can deal with them successfully if you do the three things we mentioned above: 1. Recognize the patterns. 2. Get help when you need it. 3. Be willing to change.

The Most Challenging Plateau of Growth

Finally, I want to offer a thought about getting to the $1 billion range. In my experience, no one reaches the $1 billion range without a seismic event that pushes them forward.

For example, I heard Brian Smith, the founder of Ugg, give a talk on what it took for him to get to $1 billion. He founded Ugg with $500,[4] and later sold it to Deckers Outdoor Corporation in 1996 for 14.6 million.[5] Ugg grew at an amazing rate after being purchased by Deckers, but it didn't cross the $1 billion mark until Oprah Winfrey gave away 350 pairs of Ugg shoes to her studio audience on a 2000 episode of "Oprah's Favorite Things."[6] Today the company is worth around $1.8 billion.[7]

Brian talked about the fact that few businesses can make that final leap past the $200 million range without some type of seismic event, and I agree. I have sat with many $100 million companies that every quarter return to the question, "How are we going to grow?" The bottom line is that it becomes more and more difficult to scale past $100 million, and without some event or very significant break-through, you will plateau for many years.

Your seismic event may be different, but you're going to need one to get to that level. Of course, before you do, you'll have to master the patterns that will present themselves at every previous level.

Wake-Up Call: Most businesses plateau. Do you know how to climb higher?

49

YOU HIRED TOO SOON, AND YOUR EMPLOYEE'S FAILURE IS YOUR FAULT, NOT THEIRS

I t's one of the trickiest issues to balance in business: When is the right time to add an employee? For most employers, the obvious question concerns money. Do you have enough revenue coming in to handle the additional payroll?

Yet money is usually not the key factor that will determine whether a new hire works out. Often an employee's success or failure has to do with the employer being unprepared to position the employee for success.

Often, this is a problem because the employer's enthusiasm for the hire outpaces his or her preparation for it. You've probably felt this. You start thinking about the difference it would make to have another set of hands handling certain things, and you can't wait to make it happen. In your mind, it's entirely clear what this person will do and how it will impact the effectiveness of the team.

However, that's no guarantee it will all be clear to the new employee. When a person starts a new job, it's crucial to have responsibilities and processes documented and defined. Too often, the enthusiastic employer fails to have this information ready.

You can tell this is a problem when, in the first few months, you find yourself repeating certain things:

"I'm sorry. I should have explained that to you." "My bad. I meant to go over that with you." "Don't worry, just keep at it and you'll learn that."

You find yourself saying things like this because, somewhere along the line, you got it in your head that it was okay to run a sink-or-swim type of company. I hear this all the time in my engagements: "Well, we're a sink-or-swim type of company. People here learn by doing. It's baptism by fire."

I know all this, because I ran my business for about 10 years with a sink-or-swim mentality. While some of my employees flourished in this environment early on, because they were able to swim right next to me, long term it didn't work. As the years went by and the company grew, I didn't have the time to be there beside new employees to help them, and there wasn't a system in place to give them direction. Fortunately, I had a young millennial point out the error of this thinking. I adjusted, but the legacy of that fast and loose approach to hiring and training took years to unwind. Thanks, James, for having the courage to point out that error.

That system we had was no way to onboard an employee, and that can be hard for entrepreneurs to understand. That's because the entrepreneur probably learned his or her own job in a sink-or-swim fashion. It's the nature of entrepreneurs. They figure things out. They solve problems. They relish such challenges, and they do well tackling them.

Just because you relish a sink-or-swim experience, it's a mistake to think others who come to work for you are looking for the same type of experience. Most people who apply for a job want a defined task that's a good fit for their abilities. When they're told to just figure it out, they feel like they've been left to twist in the wind. They're also not sure if they're doing a good job because you haven't made it clear what a good job is.

Even large companies often do a poor job with onboarding employees. They don't explain processes and procedures clearly.

They don't have good manuals. They don't explain the benefits, and they don't make clear what's expected.

Without a robust onboarding process, many employees come to see their job as a disorganized joke. They don't see how they're contributing to the goals of the company. It's just their J-O-B because this guy pays them $15 an hour. You're that guy. You missed your chance to make this person feel like part of the team.

Another problem with new hires is that entrepreneurs often seek to fill positions before there is enough work for a full-time employee to do. Ask the typical entrepreneur how much of his or her time it would take to do the task for which someone is being hired. They'll tell you, "Oh, I could do it in 10 hours a week."

So why do you think another person would need 40 hours? At first, Johnny, the new employee, is very busy learning things, but before long he's searching for tasks just to stay busy.

I find that it's often better to let a department get a little over-worked before you make an addition. Usually, people have more capacity than they think, and this is how you can ensure that a new employee does have enough to do.

I've seen companies, both large and small, make this mistake. They bring on an employee who just can't quite grasp the tasks or the role, and the employee usually gets the blame. "Well, Johnny just didn't cut it." That's a harsh statement since Johnny never had a chance, because the company's culture didn't include the type of onboarding or support he needed.

I have to tread lightly on this topic when I'm coaching. If I tell someone they have to work on their company culture, I know what the response will be: We have a great culture! I know, it's just that you're a sink-or-swim company, and too many of your employees are sinking as a result.

If you want to avoid problems like this, there are three questions you should ask before you make a hire:

1. If someone started on this job today, would you know how to describe the job and train them to do it?

2. If you were doing this job, how many hours a week would it take you? Why assume it would take someone else longer?
3. Are you ready to offer the new employee a world-class onboarding experience?

As you consider your onboarding experience, keep in mind I'm not talking about having a phone and computer ready on the first day (you obviously need that). I'm also not talking about having a nice welcome gift and lunch with the CEO (that's also important). I'm talking about the training and instruction necessary to get acclimated to the job they will be doing, and possibly training for the job as well. To onboard well, you need a detailed process that takes a new employee and makes him or her a productive member of the team. Great companies do this, and they reap all the benefits that most entrepreneurs unfortunately miss.

I realize that not every hire turns out great, and some people aren't going to succeed no matter what you do. However, if you don't get these basic things right, that's on you, not on them. And you have the power to do what's necessary to fix that before you make another hire.

Wake-Up Call: Most companies do not fully onboard staff well. Create a process that helps the new employee to become a productive member of the team.

50

GENERATION X: THE FIRST DIGITAL LEADERSHIP GENERATION

This chapter is for all my brothers and sisters in the most awesome generation. – Love you, Generation X

———

Generation X has waited a long time to assume the mantle of corporate leadership in America, and for the people of this generation, their time is largely here. The baby boomers are retiring and leaving the work force, and that means we're now getting the first generation to take the reins with a real understanding of the digital landscape. Except . . . not exactly.

Generation X is not like your grandparents, many of whom were flummoxed by email. The X-ers don't resist technology, and they don't sit around complaining that things were better when people wrote letters. They recognize the value of the digital revolution, and they're mostly comfortable with it.

Even so, the X-ers are not the first truly digital generation to assume corporate leadership for the simple reason that they're not digital natives. Millennials, on the other hand, are true digital natives.

Generation X is the last generation that changed the TV channel by hand. It's the last generation that actually did mail letters to friends. It's the last generation that still thinks of a phone as mainly a thing you use to make calls, as opposed to an all-purpose device that you can pretty much use to run your entire life.

It's not that Generation X doesn't get it. They get it. However, their frame of reference is entirely different from that of millennials. As digital natives, millennials have never known anything except a highly technological world. Each generation's frame of reference will influence the way that generation thinks about business and life.

Generation X remembers when the internet was a revolutionary innovation, changing everything. They remember when buying things from a computer screen — rather than going to a store and picking it out by hand — was not even a concept anyone could grasp. While they've adapted to the digital age, the point is that they had to adapt. The first generation to take leadership of corporate America with a knowledge of all things digital will also be the last generation to remember what it was like in the analog age.

What that means is that Generation X leaders, by and large, still operate with a default analog mindset. It's how they grew up thinking, and it's what comes most naturally to them. That is neither good nor bad, but it will definitely impact the leadership practices of Generation X.

For example, Generation X may prefer a face-to-face meeting or a phone call rather than a text. Hey, in 1995, if you needed to talk to someone, you just called them! You didn't text to see if they were free to talk. Millennials may find it rude, but the Gen X-ers know it's how we did things for the better part of a century.

Generation X and millennials have different frames of reference that impact their attitudes toward technological advances. Consider Slack. This new platform is becoming very popular, and it's considered by many a next-step advance beyond email. It allows for more group discussions, in real time, and easier sharing of information. The inventors of Slack clearly believe they've created something that can make email obsolete, and much of the millennial generation agrees with them.

To Generation X, this is insanity. Why would we need something to replace email? It's way better than snail mail, and we've all got it installed on our computers. We all understand it, and we're all used to it.

Generation X looks at Slack and asks, "Why do we need to use Slack?"

The millennials respond: "Why the heck aren't you using Slack?"

The generational perspectives help make both questions understandable. Email was a huge leap forward when it burst on the scene in the mid-1990s. It was a real challenge for everyone to get used to it, and it totally changed our way of communicating with each other, both in our personal lives and in our businesses. Before email, there were courier services who would make good money driving documents from place to place because people needed information right away.

To Generation X, adapting to email was a once-in-a-lifetime heavy lift. They figure that should do them for the next 100 years or so.

To millennials, however, email might as well be 1,000 years old. They don't care that it's better than letters because they have no memory of letters. They're looking for the next advancement, and that's good. You don't want a generation that isn't interested in advancement and progress.

As Generation X assumes leadership, with the millennials nipping at their heels, it's important for Gen-X to question some of its own assumptions — about the way work should be done, and about the ways people interact with each other in the business world. There's something to be said for preserving longstanding practices that are in danger of being lost to technology.

However, not everything you remember as the best is necessarily still the best, and not everything is dumb just because it's a fad. Generation X needs to combine three things to become one of the greatest leadership generations ever — its historical knowledge, its ability to adapt, and a willingness to hear what the next generation has to say. Gen-Xers could lead an amazing transition in busines, and they could set things up beautifully for the millennials to eventually take charge.

Why is all this important? It is critical to know yourself and to know others. While this is only a short summary of the differences of the two primary generations in business today, it is intended to start a discussion. The Boomers are mostly out of the workforce, so we can stop blaming them.

Generation X and millennials can be a powerhouse, if we embrace what makes both of them so unique and strong. I'm a Gen Xer through and through, so I'm happy to say that it is time for Gen X to lead. And I'm excited to see the dramatic changes we could see in the next 15 years as the last analog generation takes over in a mostly digital era.

Wake-Up Call: Generational differences are real; pretending they are not only makes them worse.

51

WE ALL MAKE MISTAKES MANAGING PEOPLE: HERE ARE TWO OF MY BIGGEST

F or some reason, managers like to run away from the word *manager*. Maybe they think it makes them sound too authoritarian, which is why they gravitate toward more positive-sounding words like *leader*.

However, there's nothing inherently negative about managing, and any business leader has to embrace the fact that – on one level or another – you are managing people. That seems so fundamental, it shouldn't even need to be said.

Yet maybe the reason people shy away from the role of manager is that it's the one area where your mistakes are most difficult to shake. When you make a budgetary mistake, you just re-run the numbers, and it's fixed. When you make a product design mistake, you go back and redesign it, and the product works.

However, when you make a mistake dealing with people, the objects of your mistake remember. Your mistake could affect their lives. They can tell others about it. It can affect your reputation.

A bad product design or a flawed budget can't look at you like you're an idiot. A person can. So, we're a little more sensitive about the mistakes we make managing people, and maybe we're a little less willing to openly talk about them, but we need to.

Nothing teaches us more than our mistakes, and we all make them. The longer you remain in business, the more you should be able to gain wisdom from these mistakes and learn to do better. However, that's not going to happen if you pretend nothing you did while managing people was ever a mistake.

So, I'll start. Earlier in my career, there were two very problematic areas that created trouble when I was managing people. The first was gossip. I know this is awful – not just as a management practice but as general human behavior – but it's long been a weakness for me. I love gossip. I love jawboning about what's going on and who's into what. For me, it could be anything from people's clothing, to who said what, to who was seen with whom. I'm not proud of this, but I need to admit it, and I paid a serious price for it as a manager.

Initially, I saw this as a healthy distraction from the nonstop seriousness of the business. There is always something going on, things to be dealt with, and decisions to be made. It seemed like it could be healthy to allow myself and my team mental breaks to talk about trivial nonsense.

However, I soon realized a couple of things. First, I was alienating people because no one likes to be the subject of gossip. It bothered them, understandably, that the boss was getting down in the dirt and talking about them like I was. I saw it as harmless and innocent, but they didn't. Second, I was causing people not to trust me. If I was the type of manager who would repeat things he'd heard to others in a careless fashion, why would anyone trust me with any information?

There was another problem that arose from my participation in gossip: I was creating a subculture of how to influence Wade. Sure, you could do it the normal way – by working hard and accomplishing your goals. However, the people in the gossip group started figuring out that they could gain my favor by letting me in on the latest juicy tidbits. It was unfair to everyone else, and needless to say, it was completely contrary to how a good manager should interact with employees.

I'm ashamed of it, and I also recognize that you can be a very mature manager and still fall into some sort of loop like this that's based on a quirk in your personality. What might that be for you? Maybe it's not gossip, but maybe you have a weakness for yelling at people. Or maybe worse things.

You should take very seriously how your indulgence in such behaviors can compromise your effectiveness as a manager. I am not suggesting there isn't any room for your true personality in your professional role, but you need to think very carefully about how things you actually do can come back to harm you and others.

My second big mistake category was promises. I was way too willing to make them – often without giving much thought to what I was promising – and not willing enough to admit before it was too late that a promise was unwise.

Here's a perfect example: I had a person working for us as a consultant, and he was doing very well in that role. But he wanted to be a sales engineer, and he was pretty assertive about asking for that opportunity. I wanted to say something encouraging to him, so I told him that if he worked hard for six months in the consulting role, I would promote him to sales engineer.

Six months came and went. I was actually on vacation with my family – stopping at a highway rest stop, if you must know – when I got a call from him. It was the six-month point, he reminded me, and I'd made him a promise.

Indeed, I had. It had not been a smart promise. He wasn't right for the sales role, and nothing he'd done in those six months had changed that. However, I didn't want to break a promise (and I was trying to get out of that rest stop), so I gave the okay for the promotion.

This was a disaster. He performed poorly in the role. I kept trying to nudge him back into consulting, but he wasn't interested in that. And the rest of the company recognized my poor business decision, which I couldn't defend with anything substantive. The fact of the matter was that I had spoken carelessly and didn't know how to back away from my words.

The move not only hurt the company by putting the wrong person in the wrong role, but it also hurt the company by undermining confidence in the CEO. Eventually the person left, and not on very good terms, while those who stayed continued to remember my mistake.

The fact is, the word promise shouldn't even be in a businessperson's vocabulary. If you want to sign contracts, that's fine. That's not the same thing because a contract spells out what's expected of both parties in an agreement that's ready to be executed. A promise is something you're committing to no matter what, and in business there's no such thing as no matter what.

Sometimes I think we make promises because we want our people to believe rewards are coming, and we want them to stay hopeful and motivated. We want them to believe we're willing to take care of them. Yet we pay a price for that when the time comes to fulfill the promise, and it doesn't make sense to do it.

We're better off laying out the circumstances in which a scenario could happen, and letting the employee know what his or her responsibility would be in making those circumstances reality. But making promises is a fool's exercise. It's every bit as foolish as gossip.

So now you can all go off and gossip about my mistakes, but before you do that, why don't you tell me something: What are some of yours? And what did you learn from them?

Wake-Up Call: We all have problem areas in our management of people, not correcting them is the biggest problem.

52

NO, YOU'RE NOT EMPOWERING YOUR EMPLOYEES WHEN YOU SAY, "I DON'T CARE"

D o business leaders need to be told that "I don't care" isn't a good phrase to use with employees?

You might think this is obvious, but you'd be surprised. Depending on the tone and the context, "I don't care" could be mistaken for an empowering phrase.

"Hey boss, what color should we paint the wall?" "I don't care!"

"Hey boss, what should we order for lunch?" "I don't care!"

The boss thinks he's empowering the employees by saying he doesn't care. He's letting them know that they're free to make whatever decision they want. Maybe that's what he's trying to do, but this isn't the way to do it.

First of all, no one wants the boss not to care — whether it's about a lunch order or the pursuit of a crucial new piece of business. That's not to say you want the boss micromanaging every decision, or that you don't want the boss trusting you to exercise your own best judgment.

Also, if you're the boss, you want to make it clear when you expect people to make their own decisions. However, consider the way people will react if they come to the boss for input on a decision, and they're told by the boss that he or she doesn't care.

One scenario might be that it's clearly the employee's job to make the decision. At least this is clear to the boss. If the employee is coming to the boss looking for direction, that could mean one of several things. One is that the employee doesn't believe the boss trusts him or her to make the call. This employee lacks the confidence to make the call for fear of what the boss will come back and say.

If this is the case, then the boss needs to make it clear: I expect you to make this decision, and I will support you when you do. "I don't care," or "Whatever," or any other similar expression, is not how you communicate that.

Maybe the employee is asking for the boss's input because he or she wants clarity on how the boss's priorities should be applied to this decision. It may not be that the employee is unwilling to make the decision, but rather he or she simply wants to double-check and make sure the decision under consideration lines up with the boss's overall thinking.

If that's the case, the boss needs to try to understand why the input is being sought, and he or she needs to make it clear that providing this input doesn't relieve the employee of the responsibility to make the decision.

If you hire people to make decisions, and they're always coming to you, then you might as well be making the decisions yourself. However, you need to respect and honor the employee's desire to clarify your thinking and priorities, even while embracing their own responsibility to make the call.

There is nothing that should happen within your company that you don't care about. That doesn't mean you have to personally seize control of every little function or detail, but you should care about what happens. And you should care about giving others the proper response to what they may be asking you. It's unsettling to your team if they get the impression that you don't care. By saying "I don't care," you may be trying to give them permission to make the decision. If you want them to make the decision, just tell them. Saying "I don't care" does not always make an employee think, "I'm being enabled to make this decision."

So, it's up to you to find clearer and more affirming ways to tell your team you trust them to make decisions. They want to make decisions that advance your vision of the company and your principles and priorities. Make it clear to them what those are.

You also need to make sure they understand that you expect them to make day-to-day decisions based on your vision and priorities, and also based on their own instincts and experience. Finally, they need to know that you'll back them up when they make decisions, because that is exactly what you hired them to do.

Wake-Up Call: You erode trust and communication when you give lazy responses to questions. Be specific on your feedback.

53

THE MENTOR DILEMMA

Today's new work force seems to want mentors more than previous generations. On first glance you might not find this particularly remarkable. Who wouldn't want a mentor? The new generation's heightened interest in mentorship tells us something beyond face value. I think it represents some serious generational differences in the way workers and bosses view management.

Remember, mentors don't train you to do your job. They share with you the experiences of having done what you're doing. They give you guidance on how to handle yourself, how to deal with people, how to pursue goals, and how to be a professional. However, they don't teach you how to perform your basic tasks.

To some degree it's the product of the fading, but not yet sdisappeared, philosophy of management known as "sink or swim." And I'll confess something to you: I used to be a sink-or-swim guy. I used to believe it was the best way to make people master their jobs.

After all, I would reason, I didn't have time to walk everyone through all the tasks they were supposed to be doing. So, it made more sense, as I saw it, to demand people know what they were doing when they walked in the door. Then those I added to the team could either prove themselves or perish. Those who remained would be an outstanding group.

A charitable way to describe this is "hands-off management." Such a manager reasons that he or she is giving people the freedom to figure things out for themselves. It's a remnant of the post-World War II era, and there was a time when it made sense to me.

That stopped around 2012, when some of my younger employees persuaded me that they'd be a lot more effective if they at least had processes or systems that established how they should do things. Without this, everyone was kind of making it up for themselves, and the results were not consistent.

One of the most successful retail establishments in the world is the Apple store. It's also the most process driven. Everyone there is intensely trained on the Apple way of doing everything — from dealing with customers to solving problems and every other aspect of the experience. The process becomes intrinsic, and that's what makes the results so predictable and so consistently good. There's no sink-or-swim if you work at an Apple store.

My young employees told me they wanted mentorship. They just needed some dependable guidance on how to do their jobs — the sort of thing a sink-or-swim manager is never going to give them.

That doesn't mean there's no value to mentoring. Of course, there's tremendous value to it. A mentor can help you understand your challenges and provide someone to listen and answer questions. Who wouldn't want that?

However, there are traps involved with mentoring. Traditionally, it's the sort of thing you see managers or senior-level people do. You want to be a good mentor and be there for people, but at some point, you have to do your job and they have to do theirs.

Also, a senior person who gets involved with mentoring should understand that the process is both upstream and downstream. If you're doing mentoring right, you should learn as much from the mentees as they learn from you. That's a real benefit for the aging portion of the workforce who are being asked by younger workers for mentors.

I would also advise this to any company that wants to start a mentorship program: Don't overthink it, don't over-invest in it, and don't try too hard to be like the biggest companies who have done it successfully. Don't waste time looking around for the perfect mentorship program to emulate.

Just get it started. This is one of the few times I'll tell you that, because I'm a big believer in systems and processes. In this case, you're running the risk of too many people trying to build the system and making it completely unwieldy. Mentorship doesn't have to be complicated. Find the people who are well-equipped to do it, and let them become the mentors.

A great example of a company effectively utilizing the just "get it started" mantra is Alcoholics Anonymous, or A. A., and the 12-step process. A. A. has thousands of groups around the U. S. and around the world, and they are only run by a very small organization. They have approximately 2 million members as of 2020,[1] and only $16 million in operating income annually![2] That means they help 2 million people at only $8 a person. That is unheard of, and that is because the system is very simple. And the groups self-manage and self-direct. A. A. has minimal oversight in local groups. This allows them to grow faster and to help more people. Of course, there are rogue groups out there and sometimes this system doesn't get it right, but, overall, many people have been helped by A. A. That would not have happened if the organization had built a big system with lots of processes and rules. Mentorship is the same. Give people some basic rules and outlines, and turn them loose. Trust me, it'll be better!

A good way to get people started is to have them read *The Coaching Habit* by Michael Bungay Stanier.[3] It's a simple and quick read, and it will give any mentor a good foundation for how to get started.

By the way, it's usually assumed the mentors have to be senior people and the mentees have to be more junior. That's a good model, but it doesn't always have to be that way. Bilateral or team mentoring can also be very effective. Colleagues can do a great job of mentoring each other because they understand better than anyone what their challenges are.

So, I'm all about mentoring. However, when you hear your people asking for mentors, make sure it's not their way of bemoaning a lack of guidance, systems, and processes to help them perform their basic tasks. They might not even realize that's what they're missing, but as their manager, you should realize it.

Give staff members what they need to do their jobs, and give them good mentoring. You'll be creating the space where they can do their jobs themselves, and you can't hope for a much better management triumph than that.

Wake-Up Call: Stop making mentorship complicated. Start a simple program today, and watch it succeed.

54

THE LAW OF THE LID

R ecently, Jeff Bezos announced he would no longer be the CEO of Amazon. Instead, he will become the executive chairman.

In my opinion, Bezos realized that it would be better for someone else to lead the company. He had reached his limit for his ability to positively impact and grow his company.

Bezos did mention that his responsibilities with Amazon were very time consuming. In an email about the change, he stated, "When you have a responsibility like that, it's hard to put attention on anything else."[1] He told his employees that he wanted time to focus on the "Day 1 Fund, the Bezos Earth Fund, Blue Origin, The Washington Post, and [his] other passions."[2]

In my opinion, these other organizations in Bezos's life also impacted his decision to leave, along with reaching his cap as leader of Amazon. One of the hardest things for leaders, CEOs, and entrepreneurs to do is to recognize that they have hit their caps, or the lids of their jars. John Maxwell, a leadership guru, calls this the "Law of the Lid."[3]

Most leaders never recognize when they've hit the lid of the jar.

Instead, they blame other people, and their businesses don't grow. They stagnate, and the "Law of the Lid" is one of the biggest reasons businesses stagnate. Leaders very seldom recognize this and put themselves in the position where someone else can be brought in to grow the business for them. It's very rare that you are blessed with the traits that allow you to start a business and then grow the business the way that Bezos did.

You can be very good at starting a business, but you're not good at running it long term. Other people are good at running businesses long term, but they aren't good at starting them. Some people are better at being entrepreneurs, and other people are better at being professional managers.

Some people do have the ability to start at zero and go all the way to a billion in revenue. For example, Bill Gates, Jeff Bezos, Sara Blakely (founder of Spanx), and Jamie Kern Lima (founder of IT Cosmetics) were able to start companies and turn them into billion-dollar businesses.

One of my most regrettable mistakes was not seeing this in my own business. There was a point when we plateaued, and I knew my leadership and ability were a big part of that stagnation. It is hard as a founder and entrepreneur to realize that you have hit the lid of your current potential.

For a year or two, I looked for other reasons why we had maxed out our potential as a business — without really considering that it could be my ability as an entrepreneur. The good news is, with some outside support, I was able to start growing again as a leader. As John Maxwell describes it, I was able to take off the lid, but it took some help. While I was able to move past that stagnation in the business, I never really recovered from the stall of the few years of not facing the real issue — me as the CEO.

I want to encourage all leaders from the CEO down to the frontline manager to learn from my example. While it is never too late to remove the lid and start growing again, a significant stall can come with a significant cost — sometimes even your job or business. It is critical to have people and tools around you to measure your growth and to ensure that if you hit the lid of your potential, you get the support and help you need to continue to grow. Or, you need to find another leader that can pick up where you have to leave off.

I have seen far too many founders that have the desire to go from zero dollars to a billion dollars. It's a dream most business owners have when they start. Although we did mention some CEOs who had the ability to start from zero and achieve wild success, the hard reality is that very few humans have the skills to make that kind of growth actually happen.

There is no hard and fast rule, but as a rule of thumb, I believe companies should take a close look at their founders when they reach $10 million in annual revenue and again when they reach $100 million. Can these founders continue to grow with this business? Do they have the skills needed? Do they have the charisma?

If you don't take these questions seriously, you will do more damage to the companies. These rules apply even more to a family business, especially for those leaders in the second or third generations. These are hard questions to ask, and very few people want the hit on their egos, but I hope you can handle it.

Wake-Up Call: Very few founder entrepreneurs have the ability to grow past $10 million in revenue. Far less have the ability to grow past $100 million. Assume you can't — without help.

Red Wagon Advisors is a great place to get these tools and assessments to help you overcome the lid on your jar.

55

WHO IS ON YOUR BUS?

L et's be honest, the past couple of years have been rough for businesses. I know many employees and employers have been anxious about all the changes and challenges that they've faced recently. There is a sense of insecurity and fear for many, and this reminds me of a time in 2004 when the business that I was in hit a downturn.

Unfortunately, we had a business unit that wasn't doing well, which meant we were faced with some hard decisions. We had to move forward without that business unit. It was tough, and I know that there are other businesses struggling with this same issue as they head into this new decade. And your company may be one of them. It isn't easy, I know.

After we made the decision to shut down the business unit, the challenge was that no matter how great our culture was, no matter how great the interaction we had with our employees, there was a real sense of loss and also lack of trust. On a side note, one silver lining that came from this difficult decision was that a couple of people wanted to try to do the work of this business unit on their own, and we said, "Go for it!" These people became instant entrepreneurs.

As we moved forward — despite me reassuring our employees that this was the only change — there was still an immense amount of anxiety and insecurity. We had a difficult time rebuilding trust.

I had to sit back and ask myself, "How are we going to rebuild this trust?" First, I set a BHAG (big, hairy, audacious goal) and a vision. At that time, we had this hot technology called Altiris. I decided to focus on Altiris and to focus on growing our business outside of Michigan. We were going to focus only on Altiris, and we were going to burn the ships with the other technologies. I use the term "burn the ships" because we were very serious and didn't have many other options. Sometimes when you have no other choice, that is when the best decisions are made. In this type of scenario, you get very serious very quickly.

Second, we had an all-hands meeting. I said, "Here's our BHAG we are going for, and here is the vision for how we are going to achieve it." We also had just landed the state of Indiana as a client, and we were positioned to grow.

Third, at our meeting I explained the theme we were going to follow. Our theme was based after Jim Collins's book *Good to Great,* a must-read book.[1] His book asks the question, "Who do we want on the bus?" We asked ourselves: Does this person have the right core values, the right attitudes, and the right performance? Then, we had to ask the second question Jim Collins proposed: What seats are available on the bus? We had to juxtapose these two questions — who do we want and what seats are available. Just because it's right to have someone on the bus, doesn't mean we have a seat for that person.

At this team meeting we knew we had the right people on the bus, and we had them in the right seats. To illustrate this, after we have presented the BHAG and vision, I told them, "There's a bus waiting outside. Everyone who buys into this concept, I want you to get on the bus." It was my Braveheart moment. I walked out the back door, and I wondered, "Will they actually follow me?" I didn't even look back.

While I walked, I just prayed that I wouldn't be in the parking lot alone.

Slowly people started following me. Then, the line moved faster as people realized there was a bus outside, and they started to eagerly hop on the bus. Everyone got on the bus! On our way to a company lunch, I got on the bus microphone, and I explained why every person was on the bus. I explained what role the person had and what role that person was going to have. The distrust and anxiety began melting away, and there was a significant uptick in the culture after that moment. At lunch, I saw people laugh and have fun for the first time in months. I knew in that instant that things had changed. Yes, the speech helped, but what made the difference was what Jim Collins taught us: Get people in the right seat. When I told them WHY they were in that seat, that was the difference maker. Years later, people still talked about the day we got on that bus.

Even as I write or tell this story today, the hair stands up on the back of my neck. It is so simple, but it is one of the proudest and scariest moments of my life.

The vision that I shared inspired the people on that bus, and they became incredibly productive. They achieved their goals for that quarter and many quarters after that.

Now you may ask, "Who cares about what you did 17 years ago?

Who cares about your Braveheart moment?"

I hope you realize we can't have Braveheart moments every quarter, but every quarter we can set goals and have an all-hands meeting. We need to share the vision for each quarter and how it relates to the BHAG. We all need to be marching in one direction.

Get out there and announce your BHAG and your vision every quarter. Follow these three principles:

First, set a BHAG and a vision.

Second, have an all-hands meeting to share your BHAG and vision. This cannot be merely an email you send out to everyone. You need to set up a well-organized and well-planned meeting. We want to see and hear people, and it's easier to communicate that way.

Third, use a theme — like having the right people on the bus —

to spark buy-in from employees. Themes are critical for the success of the meeting. When everyone on the team — or on the bus — is committed to the vision, productivity goes up, and that's when great things start to happen.

> Pro Tip: You don't get many Braveheart moments in business, and they are hard to recreate. For years, I tried to recreate a moment like that, and finally I gave up. I would recommend you do the same. Those points in time are very rarely preplanned or scripted. Looking back, our moment seems perfect, but it was not planned. We needed to get everyone to lunch, so we rented a bus. It all just came together. Those magic moments in business, those Braveheart turning points, are almost always organic. Don't go looking for them; just keep showing up and making a space for them to appear. Trust me, I tried, and you can't make them or plan them.

Wake-Up Call: Listen to Jim Collins's question: You may have the right people on the bus, but are they in the right seats?

56

THE COMPANY THAT FALLS BACKWARD
BECAUSE OF FAILED DNA TRANSFER

M any companies hit a plateau when reach about 50 employees. There are many reasons for that, but I want to focus on one of the most common.

They plateau – or worse, they go backward – because at that level the company fails at DNA transfer.

Just so we're understanding terms, DNA transfer is when the vision and fundamental drive of the company founder is passed on to another level of management. This tends to go fairly well the first time it happens – usually when the company hits 10 or 15 employees. That's because the founder himself or herself trains and equips the first level of management below him or her.

It makes sense that it would go well at this point. No one knows or embodies the vision of the company like the founder. No one can do a better job of both teaching and exemplifying how leadership in the company should work.

However, when the company hits 50 or so employees, now it's time for that level of managers to appoint the next group, and this is where the process so often breaks down.

It's not that the new group of managers is trained improperly. It's that, most of the time, new managers are not trained at all. People are simply promoted, and responsibility is delegated to them, without any effective DNA transfer to show them how to do what they're being asked to do.

Now you have people in charge of managing others, but they don't have the knowledge or the direction to know how to do it effectively. Even worse, upper management often has no idea it's a problem until it's already set the company back. After all, they think they did their jobs by delegating. They probably can tell themselves with a straight face that they "empowered" this new level of management.

However, the new managers don't have real authority. They don't know how to make sure the company's vision and core values are being honored. They don't understand what the company's core priorities are or why the company has them.

This new group of managers has two major problems working against them: They are inexperienced, and they were not trained by the founder. As a result, they're simply not going to be as good at management as the group above them, who *were* trained by the founder. The group who successfully received a DNA transfer from the founder can manage competently. However, these competent managers have no idea how to train the next group or make up for the next group's lack of experience.

Imagine being a manager under these conditions. You're poorly trained. You have limited experience. And the manager above you keeps butting into what you were told was going to be your job. How can you possibly succeed under these conditions?

Few could, and this is where backward momentum is a real threat to the company. The culture the founder nurtured can disappear. Drama becomes common. The small company that the founder used to be able to lead so effectively becomes an out-of-control entity, because there are too many pockets and situations in which it's not clear who's in charge. Those who do try to manage can't do so effectively. It's a mess.

Too many entrepreneurs misdiagnose the problem at this point.

They'll identify a few people who are doing well and lament that they can't find more people like that. You will typically hear the founder say at this stage, "We just need to figure out how to clone the people that get it." It's a clear indication that they don't get it. The solution is not a cloning machine. That is just an excuse for poor performance from the leadership on their core job, building and transferring great culture.

Building leaders requires training, re-training, reviews, check-ins — a constant process of learning and accountability. The top leadership of the company has to work hard at it.

Yet, too many companies think they're succeeding just because they've grown big enough to need more leaders. They're at 50 employees and they decide they need another 20.

However, it's not long before one of the newly minted managers comes to the boss and says, "Look, I can maybe lead 8 or 10 people. I can't lead the 20 you've given me."

Over the long term, the result of this mistake is very predictable. We've all seen companies that were known for great service at a certain point in time. But you come back 10 years later – or maybe 20 or 30 years later – and now they have the worst service in their industry.

How did that happen? They promoted leaders without teaching them how to lead. They didn't do the DNA transfer. It worked great the first time it was done, because the founder was able to personally train the next level of leaders. However, over time that gets lost, and you walk in one day and wonder what happened to your company.

DNA is not easy to transfer, and it certainly doesn't transfer itself. The failure to do that is one of the biggest reasons so many companies can't successfully get past the $10 million or 50-employee level.

Wake-Up Call: It's not just culture; it is the transfer of culture to the frontline staff.

57

YOU KNOW THE BROKEN WINDOWS THEORY BY HEART. NOW FIX YOURS.

———

M ost people in the business world have heard the broken windows theory, but they might not know its origins.

This theory became popular when Rudy Giuliani first became mayor of New York City in 1994. As Giuliani and his team pondered how to improve the city, it occurred to them that they could make the city safer by improving the appearance of neighborhoods, or fixing their broken windows. Once neighborhoods are defaced with graffiti or broken windows, other types of lawless behavior tends to escalate. If no one cares about a neighborhood and it becomes broken down, lawlessness and disorder tend to prevail.

Giuliani and his team considered the work of George Kelling and James Wilson, criminologists who believed that minor crimes often led to more serious ones.[1] They agreed with the theory and believed that if they just focused on prosecuting the smaller crimes, the larger ones might not even occur.[2] Their efforts had dramatic results, improving the appearance of these formerly crime-ridden neighborhoods and reducing more violent crimes.[3]

Businesses watched the major transformation of New York City and learned from this. They said, "If we can identify our own 'broken windows' and fix them, we might also change our corporate atmosphere in ways that would lead to greater success."

The theory is very popular, especially considering the success it had in New York City. However, for far too many companies, it remains simply a theory. They recognize that it would help them to fix their own broken windows, but they don't actually do it. Don't be one of those companies.

Let's start with the most difficult issue to confront: Corporate leaders don't address their broken windows because it stings their egos to do so. What, after all, are broken windows in the corporate setting? They are problems that have been left far too long without being addressed. It's the ugly cables exposed in the hallway everyone walks by. It's the conference room chairs that don't match. It's that weird smell coming from the refrigerator in the break room.

These are things everyone knows are present, although you as the leader may have gotten used to them. Maybe you've accepted them and have simply said, "That's just how things are around here."

Maybe it's not just aesthetic issues. Maybe you're perpetually behind in your financial record keeping. Maybe you're always talking about upgrading your enterprise software, but you never quite get around to it.

These are the signs of a company that is not committed to excellence. Employees at a company like this tend to doubt they'll be rewarded for their initiative, innovation, and hard work. So why bother displaying laudable performance at a company that doesn't value excellence?

I have often counseled clients to be vigilant about cleaning out their refrigerators. Why? Surely there are more important issues than that to tackle.

However, at some point you've probably sent around one of those emails letting everyone know to clean their stuff out of the refrigerator by end-of-day Friday, because anything left in there is going to be tossed. Now what do you do when several employees don't clean their stuff out on Friday? You said you would toss it. Do you now think: "I don't want to throw out their stuff, so I'll give them another chance?" What happens when another chance turns into three or four chances, and you're still not throwing the stuff out?

This impacts your business in ways you may not realize. You're sending a signal to your people that you don't mean the things you say, and that they can ignore your warnings without paying a price. They'll feel the same way about project deadlines or expense reports. Sure, the boss says we're supposed to do this, but nothing happens when we don't.

By contrast, what will happen if you throw out everything in the fridge at 5 p.m. sharp on Friday? You told them you would! Now they'll expect you to mean — and back up — the things you say.

Subtle things like this can make all the difference between an atmosphere that engenders excellence and one that accepts broken windows.

So why don't companies actually do this? It starts at the top, and the person at the top is often the least likely person to recognize the broken windows. After all, he or she has been living with them a long time, and they don't seem to be causing big problems.

In order to identify the broken windows, and be in a position to fix them, you can do several things. One is to become highly critical of your own operation. Some people have the mental fortitude to pull this off, but for many others, it's a struggle. Another option is to bring in outsiders to observe your operation and point out the broken windows to you. They'll have no trouble noticing them, but it might sting when they point them out to you.

You can also ask your employees, although I'd suggest a less direct way of getting their feedback. If you simply ask your employees what your broken windows are, they might be reluctant to give you a candid answer. They might sense that you have a blind spot about certain things, and they might not be confident they can broach these subjects with you.

So instead, ask them three questions: What should we stop doing? What should we start doing? What should we keep doing?

Their answers to these questions will expose a lot of broken windows. Many of them are little things. They're not hard to fix. Companies who ignore the little things often send a message that they can't be trusted to get the big things right either — or at least not at a level of excellence.

Wake-Up Call: You are walking past broken windows in your business every day and accepting them. It's time to be serious about excellence and clean up your company.

58

WHEN THE SMART ENTREPRENEUR
KNOWS IT'S TIME TO QUIT

Let's talk about the virtues of quitting. Of giving up. I realize I'm provoking every instinct entrepreneurs have to never quit, never give up, and never admit defeat. Generally, I admire those instincts, and I even share them. I don't want to turn any of you into quitters in a general sense.

However, many of us have learned from experience that you have to know when it's time to let go of certain ideas, initiatives, and priorities because they're not going anywhere. They're also keeping you from better opportunities that deserve your attention.

Let me set it up with a story from my own illustrious sports career. When I was a teenager, my parents moved the family to Brazil. While attending school there, I got involved with track. I was not a great runner, but I trained hard. And I did the best I could.

One of the things I learned about Brazilian culture – something very different from our sports culture in the United States – is that it was considered perfectly acceptable for a runner to simply stop running if it was clear he was not going to finish in the top three. It wasn't mandatory by any means, but most runners who could see they weren't going to finish first, second or third would simply peel off and stop running. In Brazil's culture, there was no point continuing to run if you had no chance of being one of the top finishers. Runner after runner would quit, and no one would think anything of it.

Now, with my American sensibilities, I had no interest in quitting. Even though I had no chance of finishing in the top three, I would just keep going. According to everything I had ever learned, it was important to finish and to do so as strongly as I could.

As a result, if you scan the Brazilian high school track results from the early 1990s, you will find lots of fourth-place finishes by a certain Wade Wyant. I wasn't the fourth-best runner, but I was the one who refused to stop running. Now I'm proud of my fourth-place finishes, but I didn't get anything for them. That's fine in high school sports, but it's not fine if that keeps happening to you in business.

A friend of mine had an interesting idea around 2005. He wanted to start a newspaper syndicate, and he signed about 20 contract writers who would send him content each week — so he could turn around and offer the content to newspapers all over the country.

The syndicate started with a handful of newspaper subscribers and seemed to have potential. However, soon after that, the newspaper industry started suffering under financial pressure, and my friend was never able to grow the syndication business. For six years he tried, making just a few hundred dollars every month while his other lines of business paid the bills. Finally in 2012, he received a big piece of business from a major client, and he realized he could only handle the new business if he let go of the syndicate.

In retrospect, he says he probably should have let it go three or four years earlier, but he was proud of the lineup he'd put together and the content they put out every day. He didn't want to give up on the idea, even though the numbers suggested he should.

When was the last time you did an honest, candid assessment of everything you're doing, and made tough decisions about whether some of it should be put aside?

It's hard to do, especially when you've invested time and money in it, and there's always the entrepreneur's instinct to "run it out," just like I ran out those races in Brazil. Still, you need to look for clues that might tell you a certain idea simply isn't going anywhere. You need to ask some hard questions.

One is simply this: Do you still have the passion for this that you had when you started it? If you don't, then you're just running it out. You're trying to do the right thing, but you might not be doing the smart thing.

That brings us to a second point: Do you find yourself using the language of "doing the right thing" with respect to this idea? Do you find yourself saying things like, "I'm going to see this through," and "I refuse to give up"?

No one talks that way about something that's working. No one needs to. So, if you are, you need to look yourself in the eye and ask why it's come to that.

Often in this situation, your subconscious already knows what the score is. In its own way, the subconscious is screaming at you, "This isn't gonna fly!"

However, you're proud of the idea, and you're invested in it. At some point you probably told a lot of people about it, and they saw how excited you were. It's hard to come back later and admit you had to give up on it.

Some years ago, I was running a business I had started with some partners. It was a struggle, but our most significant issue was a broken partnership. Not wanting to disappoint anyone or give up early, I was determined to see it through. Then came the day when my partners sat me down and told me they were firing me, and they were buying me out. I would not have the opportunity to run this out. It was over.

I remember sitting in my car after it happened, watching all the remaining board members walk into the business to take over for me.

I felt relief. I realized I'd just been running it out, and I realized that I would almost certainly move on to something very soon that would be a better fit for me. To be clear, that is not to say I wasn't disappointed and angry. I could write a book on bad partners and partnerships, but that will be another day. In the end, when I did a candid recap of my role as CEO in that business, I realized that I was done. I should have pulled the plug myself.

This is a painful thing to write about. To make it a little better and to have a good laugh, this time I came in third, not fourth. However, it was still not winning, and I got fired.

No one is saying you should give up on an idea after six months, or that you should quit at the first sign of trouble. Anything you try is going to involve challenges, and you should expect to fight through those challenges if you're going to succeed at anything.

However, there comes a time when, if you can be objective, you should see that your best move is to move on to something else. It's hard to be objective when the idea was yours, and you once had big plans for it.

Yet, these are the kinds of decisions successful entrepreneurs must learn to make. I don't want you to be a quitter; I just want you to understand when it's time to quit.

Wake-Up Call: It may be time to give up — on the wrong things.

59

YOUR BOARD MEMBERS: IT'S TIME TO MAKE THEM 10 YEARS YOUNGER

I don't want to assume your company has a board – whether formal directors or a less-formal board of advisors – but I will tell you this: If you don't have one, you should.

The presence of a board is evidence of your maturity as a company. There's no reason for why it's "not the right time" or whatever else CEOs say. You know a lot, but you don't know everything. And you can't possibly consider every perspective that might bring value to your business strategies.

That brings me to my real point: If you've got a board, especially if it consists of people who were recruited for their many years of experience, you should consider refreshing its membership. Specifically, you should try to lower the average age on your board by 10 years.

Now this comes with caveats, of course. If the average age of your board members is 35, I don't want you getting a bunch of 25-year-olds. People who are young have great energy and great ideas, but experience counts for a lot. You want people on your board who have been around and have seen a few things.

However, there's a balance between experience and fresh perspective. If you have lots of the former but too little of the latter, you're not getting the value you could be getting out of your board.

At many companies, the typical board members are in their 50s and 60s. That's not hard to understand. People who get recruited to boards tend to have serious experience in corporate leadership. By the time you reach a position like that, and then serve in it for a while, you often find yourself in your 50s and 60s.

However, if you look at a person's perspective on business issues, there's a huge difference between the way a 57-year-old thinks and the way a 47-year-old thinks. The 57-year-old probably entered the workforce in the mid-1980s. email didn't exist. Websites didn't exist. E-commerce didn't exist. By the time these things came along, your 57-year-old board member had grown comfortable with the old system and probably struggled to get accustomed to the new one.

That same 57-year-old entered a business world with ideas about customer service, personnel policies (they didn't call it human resources back then) and product development that are very different from the ideas of today.

The 47-year-old entered the workforce in the 1990s. By the time he or she got into upper management, it was at least a decade later. So, the 47-year-old has come up in a world that's much more progressive in its use of technology, in the way it connects to customers, and in the way it thinks about growth strategies.

The experience of the older board members is still valuable, of course, but sometimes you have to balance experience with fresher insight.

Recently, I heard from a friend about a client who produced a film documentary. The documentary is pretty good. But the client is 72 years old, and guess how he intended to distribute the film? In movie theaters.

After a year of getting nowhere with this, some younger colleagues explained how digital downloads work, and they've finally got a strategy that might earn them some money.

This particular 72-year-old has a very impressive track record in business, and he can probably offer lots of great insight to younger entrepreneurs. However, he's not up to speed on everything in the modern world, and he needed the insight of some younger people to help him devise a strategy that will work for him today.

The point here is not to minimize the value of experience. It's to find the right balance between experience and perspective. Consider the current makeup of your board, and then ask yourself: If the average age on your board was 10 years younger than it is right now, what might you gain? What current innovations or trends might those younger board members recognize and understand?

Also remember: If you're trying to grow your business, you'd benefit from the perspective of board members who have tackled the growth challenge somewhat recently. The older your board members, the further removed they likely are from their businesses' own growth periods. They may have had great success, but they might have had it in an era when growth was achieved in very different ways. The younger board members probably faced many of the same challenges and opportunities you did.

Your board members should be helping you to navigate the challenges of today's business world. The people who can do that best will have modern insights and modern attitudes — not only about business but also about society and people. Granted, when you go younger, it becomes harder to find people with the business track record that would recommend them as good board members. It will take some work to find the best people in the right age group.

Wake-Up Call: Your board needs better prospective on the challenges of today. You need a refresh of your board members.

60

WHATEVER YOU DO, DON'T ABANDON
THE FLYWHEEL

Jim Collins's flywheel concept, from his 2001 classic *Good to Great*, is one of the most iconic notions in business.[1] In fact, the concept of a flywheel was so successful that he elaborated on it in *Turning the Flywheel*.[2]

It's a simple idea: Your flywheel is the big idea, function, or critical steps that power your business's success. At first it seems impossible to get it to turn, and it takes tremendous effort to get the flywheel to make even one rotation. You keep pushing, and pushing, and pushing . . . and eventually this big heavy wheel starts turning under its own power. Now its sheer size is your friend, not your enemy, because now that you've gotten it started, it's going faster and faster and no one can stop it.

Most people don't realize the effort it took to get the flywheel turning, but you do, and that's why you truly appreciate how it's powering your success.

Your flywheel is the one thing your business does, over and over again, that makes you money. It's the primary basis for your business's existence. It's the one thing (or the one set of steps) you must stay committed to if you want to enjoy sustained, long-term success.

Yet I see a curious phenomenon among many entrepreneurs: They abandon their flywheels. It typically comes in a speech to the company about the need to diversify, or include new products or services. There is good diversity in your business model, and then there is abandoning the flywheel.

Unfortunately, in most cases when a business owner is talking about diversity, they are typically talking about abandoning that flywheel that was so hard to start. They either don't know or don't remember how difficult it was to get the momentum going with their flywheel.

When I hear this, I want to scream "Stop, don't kill the golden goose or flywheel you worked so hard to build!" I'm not saying you have to stick with a bad idea. (See my chapter on when to give up.) However, in most cases, we leave the flywheel at the wrong time or in the wrong way!

Collins says you have to keep turning the flywheel over and over to maximize its power[3]. A lot of entrepreneurs don't have the patience to do that. They'll turn it 1,000 times, which feels like a lot, but then their focus wanders. They get excited about a new idea, or they start thinking they need to reinvent the flywheel to get it to turn better or faster.

You might compare it to the mistakes inexperienced painters sometimes make. When you're painting, you know that a given stroke will often leave the paint with streaks. The experienced painter knows that if you leave the paint alone, it will moderate itself and work all the streaks out naturally.

However, the inexperienced painter might not understand that nuance, and he will keep applying more and more strokes in a frustrating and futile attempt to force the streaks out of the paint. The result is likely to be even more strokes because he doesn't understand the paint can take care of itself if he just lets it rest. This is called overworking the paint, and I refer to it often when coaching entrepreneurs.

That's the way a lot of companies treat their flywheels. They can't stop tweaking it, changing it, questioning it, and trying to redirect it. They don't understand the flywheel is gaining momentum on its own, and the best thing they can do is stay committed to it.

Now let's be clear about something: there are bad flywheels. I don't want you to stick with yours if it's hopelessly flawed. However, if your flywheel is bad, you're in trouble, because your flywheel is most likely the idea that led you to start your business in the first place. If you're already in operation and you're having to come up with a new flywheel, you've got a very difficult challenge in front of you. Coming up with a new one is better than sticking with one that's proven it won't work, but it's not a position you want to be in.

For the most part, my scenario here assumes that your flywheel is basically solid – that it aligns with your strengths and the strengths of the team you've put together. That doesn't mean you should ignore opportunities to improve it.

How do you distinguish between a helpful improvement and that manic overworking of the paint? Every flywheel is different, so it's hard to answer the question specifically, but I would say this: When you think of an improvement that excites you, because you've realized through objective analysis that it's going to take something good and make it even better, that's probably a healthy improvement. When you can't stop tweaking the flywheel because you're losing confidence or patience, now you might be setting yourself back.

Those who abandon or keep reinventing their flywheels probably don't appreciate how badly they are setting themselves back. Keep in mind: A crucial element of the flywheel concept is that it's long, hard work, at first, to get the flywheel to turn. It's only after you stick with it for a while that the flywheel starts turning faster and faster, eventually turning its size and weight into an advantage, where at first it made things very difficult for you.

What do you think will happen when you abandon the flywheel you've been pushing and go back to square one with a brand new one? Exactly. You're back at the start, and you're once again experiencing the long, hard slog of trying to get that gigantic thing to turn.

I realize this is raising a valid question: How do you pursue continuous improvement if it's such a big problem to change your flywheel?

This is where a solid change management process makes a big difference. It's the reason so many companies have adopted standards like ISO 9000. Once an organization reaches a certain size, it's dangerous if they start making changes on a whim.

There is a clear distinction to be made between mere change and real improvement, and the ISO-certified company is much more likely to a) know the difference, and b) stick with improvement.

There's an exercise I take clients through to help them understand, and stay committed to, their flywheels. I use sticky notes, and I arrange them in a big circle. Clients move them around for the purpose of ranking what they do best and what they don't do as well. Those in the latter category tend to be the constraints on the business, and this shows them the importance of minimizing or eliminating those things they don't do well.

By the time they've gone through this exercise, they've pretty much identified their flywheel. Having gone through this exercise to identify it, there's no reason they shouldn't stay committed to it over the long term.

Companies who abandon their flywheels – whether out of impatience or inexperience or lack of confidence in their own concepts – contribute mightily to the familiar statistic of most businesses failing within their first five years. There is no reason to let that happen. Just because the flywheel isn't rolling and picking up speed at first, is no reason to stop pushing.

It's the reason you started the business in the first place. It's what you do best. It's the one thing that has the most power to deliver success.

So, keep pushing, and pushing . . . and pushing. I know it's going to take time, but once it picks up speed and starts rolling, you'll be astonished by what it can do for you. At that point, you'll be glad you stuck with it.

Pro Tip: You will be stuck with your flywheel for a while. This is why starting your business correctly is so important. For many of us, this tip is too late. We already have a business and a set flywheel, even if it's not defined. For those of you thinking about a future business, take it from an old timer, and think long and hard about your flywheel. If you want real success, you'll have the same one for a long time.

Pro Tip for Multiple Flywheels: I'm often asked if you can have multiple flywheels, and the easy answer is yes. The hard thing is that you have to earn the second one. In fact, McDonald's has only one flywheel. So, before you think you've earned a second one, take a minute and then go turn the one you have a few more times. You most likely aren't ready for a second one.

Wake-Up Call: Develop and stick to one flywheel.

61

COMPENSATION DOES DRIVE BEHAVIOR, SO PAY FOR WHAT YOU WANT!

The saying "compensation drives behavior" is one of the first things I heard a sales manager say. I've also heard this mentioned over and over again within sales, and in many cases, it's true. You will often see sales compensation and strategic decisions made based on this one idea. For the most part, you'll find that business leaders agree with this statement (with some exceptions).

However, there is still a raging debate on how far it's acceptable to pay for behavior. A great example is, "If compensation drives behavior, we should tie compensation to sales reps updating CRM, or a customer relationship management system." (Technically, CRM is a part of sales since it's a tool that helps people manage their sales and contacts.)

When pushing the envelope on paying for behavior, it also leads to a very negative attitude within sales. For example. "Well, if you want us to do that, then we should be compensated for that." This is a very entertaining debate, and if you ever want to have some fun at a sales conference (late at night in the bar, preferably), toss one of those logic bombs out there, and watch the fireworks.

My desire is not to debate or make a worn-out point. I want to expand it. I don't believe you can apply this idea to everything, but I do think we should use it for more things.

Let me make the point by sharing a quick personal story. A few years ago, I spoiled my kids and bought them iPads. At that time, our family had five iPads, which could seem excessive, and I guess it is. As I'm sure you have experienced in your own home, power cords and chargers get misplaced easily, especially when dealing with pre-teen and teen children. The automatic reaction is to grab the first replacement you can find, even if it's in your brother's room. My family is no exception.

Well, this weekend my kids had somehow found a way to *lose* all five of our chargers. You can imagine my frustration that Saturday morning when I realized I could not find even *my* charger. I called an immediate family meeting with the kids (my wife stayed out of this train wreck), and I insisted that nothing would happen that morning until I had all five chargers. Then my kids went off to find the chargers. As much as I demanded they get moving, they didn't try very hard. They got distracted. After 20 minutes of looking, they had only found one.

At that moment, it struck me that compensation drives behavior. I called for an immediate regroup. "Kids, I'm giving you 10 minutes. If you bring a charger and cable to the kitchen in the next 10 minutes, you'll get a dollar for each one." You can imagine what happened.

They found six chargers, plus an iPhone charger (I didn't pay out for that one)! Not only did I get all five, but I also got an additional charger that a neighbor kid had left at our house. The best part is, I got it all in 5 minutes.

Apparently, the compensation drove the behavior, but you will notice a bonus. I made the reward time sensitive. The kids only had 10 minutes to find the chargers. When the time ran out, the offer disappeared (an apparent sales trick, but hey, it worked on them).

How powerful could the idea of compensation drives behavior be in other areas of your organization outside of sales? More importantly, how far could you push this concept to improve company performance before it does not have the desired effect, or has the baggage we see in sales?

At companies I have helped in the past, we have expanded the idea of CDB (Compensation Drives Behavior) outside of sales. They have seen a significant, measurable, and positive effect. I can't predict with certainty that it will work for you. However, I would strongly encourage you to consider it in your own organization. From the CEO down to the line manager, look for ways to apply this principle.

For the skeptics out there, think about what it would honestly cost you. If you don't have "at risk pay" today, introduce it in a small way, and measure the results. If you see positive movement, even the most conservative of managers or financial controllers will be willing to give your second program the green light. If you start small and, for whatever reason, the program doesn't work, you risk very little.

Wake-Up Call: You are not leveraging pay for performance. It's time to change that because compensation drives behavior.

62

HOW HANDWRITTEN NOTES CAN IMPACT YOUR BUSINESS

R ecently, Harvard Business Review published an article called "The Easiest Thing You Can Do to Be a Great Boss" that highlighted the need for recognition within the workplace.[1] In the article, HBR highlights the additional value most people feel when getting a handwritten note over an email. Recognizing your team is an essential area of business I think many people neglect to think about. Make it personal and write the note by hand!

This is a principle one of my first business coaches taught me early in my career. Ken Vanderberg stressed the importance of saying thank you. He also stressed the importance of writing messages by hand. I took Ken's advice, and I have actively written thank you notes for about 18 years. The HBR article caused me to pause and think back on the power of these notes. Seldom will I get direct feedback from the person that I give the letter of recognition to. Despite that fact, I always see a difference in that person's spirit and attitude.

I took this principle a step further as I matured in my career and as my business grew. We started a tradition early in the company to have a corporate meeting and holiday party right after Christmas.

The first few years we began holding this get-together, I decided to do something bigger than just write a note to "high performers" on the team. I decided to follow the Jim Collins's principle of having the right people on the bus.[2] We had recently downsized, and I wanted to make a point to the team that we had the right people on the bus. So, a few weeks before Christmas, I wrote a personal holiday card for each employee.

These cards didn't just say, "Merry Christmas! -Wade." For each card, I spent time thinking about something the person had done that year and thanking them for it. More importantly, I would try to find something to highlight at work, or in their lives, that I was excited about for the coming year.

I still remember the joy it brought them and me. Every holiday party, the room was abuzz, but one of the main topics was my notes. People asked each other, "Did you get a card with a note from Wade?" and "What did it say?" (I tried to be sincere but also funny.) As I would look around the room, I could see my partners and other executives in the business cringe as people talked about how cool it was. They could have easily done the same thing any year, but they never took the time.

This yearly holiday card became a tradition, and now I send one to every employee, every year. I have also expanded that to suppliers and friends of the business. I can tell you it is a ton of work, but it always pays off. The key to the real value is this – you can't just sign your name to a generic note. You have to say something personal, and the other person has to believe you thought about it. This is so easy, and I would encourage everyone to try to send at least one hand-written note a week.

My only regret on this subject is that it took me 18 years to send one to my first coach — the one that gave me the idea. Thanks, Ken. Your handwritten note is in the mail.

Wake-Up Call: Show more gratitude in your business, and do it via handwritten notes.

63

BEING HELD HOSTAGE IN YOUR OWN BUSINESS

I recently had a friend call me with a problem. She had an IT professional who knew a lot about her company because he had worked for her for a number of years, and he was demanding a raise.

To make matters worse, he wasn't sharing any of the critical information about the infrastructure that he had built, and he had all the passwords. Since he felt that he was in control, he insisted on, rather than asked for, a pay increase. My friend said, "Well, let's talk about this."

However, the individual who was holding her hostage said, "You know there's nothing to talk about. You just need to trust me." She was being held hostage in her business.

It reminded me of all the times that I have seen this in business. This is an extreme example. In most cases, the examples are more subtle, so we actually give in to these hostage takers.

I remember the first hostage taker I ever saw. It was back in 2003, and we were working with a regional bank. I had not seen this phenomenon before, because I had only been in business for about 10 years at this point.

My team and I went to visit this fast-growing bank to talk about implementing some of our technology into their system. It was a nice meeting with some very intelligent people, but they said, "We need to wait for George." (Obviously, that's not his real name.)

I said, "That's fine, we'll wait for George."

After a few minutes of small talk, George finally showed up, but he had a nasty attitude. He came in there and abused everyone in the room. In a gruff voice, he said, "What's this meeting about? Why are we here?"

In response, the other members asked my team to give a presentation, and we did. However, George continued his abusive behavior. He said, "Well, that's not going to work here."

Surprisingly, everyone just defaulted to what George said.

I thought, "This is weird." So, I asked some questions: "George, What's your role in the business?"

In a pompous and arrogant voice, he said, "I'm the lead technician here."

In the room there was a manager and a vice president, yet everybody acquiesced to George, the lead technician.

After he left, I tried to get to the bottom of it. I asked, "What's George's main job? What does he do? What's his role?"

"Well, George is our visionary. He has to help us figure out what technology we need."

I asked, "Why is that?"

"George built all the technology here, and we really need him."

George had basically pushed these guys into a corner and had forced them to give him a special role. Then, he would go into meetings and dictate what they were and were not going to do. They all listened to him because no one wanted to cross George. He knew the systems, and he could pull the plug at any moment if he chose to. He was literally holding this company hostage and making all the decisions.

By the way, this is not just an IT problem. We see this in sales and in operations, too. In fact, sales is where I see it the most, and it is where I have personally experienced the worst of it. This scenario happens in all parts of the business.

Here are a few signs that you're being held hostage in a business:

- You can't start a meeting without this person.
- You can't make a decision without his or her input.
- Everyone has to default to this person.
- Everyone else is stepping on eggshells.
- This person can be very abusive, but is defended and protected.

You know you've got a potential hostage taker if you fear this person will leave. If you have a destructive person — but you can't let them leave — you have a hostage taker, especially if this person has some knowledge or capabilities in your business that force you to give in to him or her.

I have seen this type of situation played out far too often. While I can't promise you that everything will be okay if you let this person go, I can promise you one thing: over the long run, you will have a significant gain. This has been the case in every scenario that I have seen. You may run into some problems. He or she may make things difficult for you. I know there will be pain in the short term, but in the long term, your business will benefit from the decision to let this person go. You should never keep an abusive person. They are Just Toxic.

We typically see these hostage takers in smaller businesses, and they have to be moved out, especially as the business gets bigger. Everyone else in the business is being affected by this person and not growing as a professional, because the others are relinquishing all their decision-making capabilities to the hostage taker.

I am telling you an important truth: Do not negotiate with hostage takers. There's no room in your business for these dangerous and destructive people. Move these people out of your business. It's the only way that they will learn. Once they've progressed to the point of hostage taking, you can't convince them to change their minds.

Wake-Up Call: Stop wasting your time on abusive people. It's time to let them go.

64

THE ANATOMY OF SEPARATION FROM A TOXIC OR POORLY PERFORMING EMPLOYEE

———

The word "firing" is old school, and it's not appropriate today. In the modern world, employees are not under contract, and in most states, neither are employers — unless you work for a union. Most employment is an at-will arrangement, so you are talking about a separation. We have to change the terminology we use. While the person who is being let go may want to use the term "fired," the reality is that it's a separation between two entities — a person and a business. It's best to use the words "separation event" instead of "being fired."

In my experience, more employees initiate separation events than businesses. Far more people leave businesses than are asked to leave businesses. However, the right to separate goes both ways. Just like the employee has the right to separate from the employer, the employer has the right to separate from the employee.

Why am I taking the time to write what is commonly known? Well, it is not commonly practiced. There is a stigma with a business separating from an employee, because it is seen as a negative. Yet there is very little stigma in an employee leaving a business. While

I'm not advocating for businesses to separate from their staff without significant thought and consideration, I am strongly advocating for businesses to do it more often. In our current culture, "firing" a staff member has so much stigma that bad members of a team stay around far too long. It is hurting business, and in the end, it is hurting the rest of the team that is performing or has a great attitude.

I hope this final chapter in the book will help you overcome that stigma and fast track your A players, or best-performing team members.

Psychological Hurdles to Overcome

Here's the first psychological hurdle you have to overcome: When you do have to separate from an employee, and it's your choice, and not theirs, remember that employees are making this choice far more often than you are. In many cases, they would probably like to separate from you, but they can't, or they just won't take the time to do it. I always reassure employers that this person could separate from you at any time they want to. And while it is very important that you need to do the right thing, you can't shy away from a separation event.

In this capitalist system that we live in, if a better opportunity came along for this employee, he or she would have no problem separating from you. For example, in my last business, I was an owner, but not the only owner, and I was the CEO. If I had been offered a better role in a prestigious organization, I would have left the company. Employees at all levels of the business, not just the front level, are willing to leave for a better opportunity. We must change the guilt that employers feel about the separation. Employees do not feel that same level of guilt about separating from employers.

Preparation for the Separation Event

Before you have a separation event, you need to prepare for it. The legal liability for the separation event is primarily on the employer. The money you spend on talking to an attorney about an upcoming separation event is worth every penny. It's not just the cost of a separation event going poorly that must be considered, it's the time, the public relations nightmare, and the culture hit that could occur if the separation event goes poorly.

Talk with an attorney and have one involved with almost all of the separation events for your company — unless you are talking about a part-time staff member. However, even with a part-time employee, I would think about it.

Since I am not an attorney and don't give legal advice, talk to your attorney before you prepare for any separation event and before acting on anything I have said in this article.

Principle 1: Separation Agreement with Severance Package

There will always be an exception to this rule, but whenever I have a separation event, I want to create an agreement between me and the person who is leaving that states that he or she is agreeing to leave. I give the person a severance package for that agreement.

What do I mean by that? You have the right to separate from anybody at any moment without cause in most states. But it's a lot easier if you work with an attorney and draft a separation agreement with some type of severance for the person's agreement not to hold you liable and that this is a separation that he or she agrees to.

It seems awkward and difficult at first, but I've been doing this for 25 years, and this is my preferred way to handle a separation. I've done it, and I've had it done to me. I'm a big believer that it's just a clean break for everybody. If you're having a separation and there isn't fraud, gross negligence, or some significant issue, this is the way I like to do it.

Small caveat: Most human resources attorneys tell you to build a list of issues against the person, but I don't like that. It turns the whole thing into a negative situation. Then you must explain to them why you fired them.

I would rather say, "This is not working. It doesn't make sense to get into why. Here's an agreement. If you choose not to take the agreement, then we'll go down a different path, which is ugly for both of us." The reality is that the situation will always be ugly for anyone who doesn't agree to the severance package and the terms you have offered.

I've handled separation events many times. Attorneys don't always agree with me about choosing to not build a case against the person, but I've completed many of these events with an attorney's help, and I've never had a separation event go sideways on me.

Principle 2: Think about the Logistics of the Separation

In our highly digital world, you need to think of all the downstream impact of a separation event. In the past, you brought them to your office and fired them. Afterwards, they just cleaned off their desks and left. However, in the past, employees didn't have accounts with different web services. They didn't have login information and passwords and digital solutions that were part of their jobs.

In the current scenario, they have all types of connections — laptops, phones, emails, and web services. In smaller and mid-market companies, they don't always think about all the logistics involved in a separation. The logistics of separating from someone today are more complicated than 10 to 20 years ago. What are all those connections that need to be addressed? Some of the downstream effects you'll never be able to deal with, so you have to expect some collateral damage from the separation.

Principle 3: Humans Are Psychological

Since humans are psychological, there are various complexities involved in dealing with them, especially when it comes to separation. It's not like the movies where you say, "Today's your last day. Have a nice day." Then the person walks out. It's a different experience.

Unless you are dismissing them for gross negligence or fraud, you owe it to that human who has been on your team to walk them through these steps with dignity. However, you don't owe them a two-hour explanation. It's critical — no matter how seasoned you are — that you have a coach or an attorney who walks you through the different complexities of a separation. You want to make sure that a separation event is handled properly, and you don't miss an important step.

Some people want to know what they could have done differently or better. They want to know what was wrong. Even if it would help them — and it would not help them to tell them that at that moment

— it opens you up to significant risks and liability issues. It's not a conversation I like to have.

I tell people, "In this moment, your focus has to be on what's next for you. If you focus on us or the business, you're wasting energy that should go into what's best for you and your family." You owe it to that person to keep bringing them back to that.

That person will also have a lot of questions, such as, "What do I do about email? What about my health care? What do I do if I need help finding another job?" Those are three of the primary questions I see — technology questions, HR questions, and employment questions. I like to have someone lined up ready to help that person. I tell them, "Here's your IT person and your HR person. They're both expecting your call. And here's a firm or individual who we've arranged to help you make a new resume."

Some people think, "If you're separating from that person, why would you go through all that?" If you have the capability of making this a smooth separation, it's in your best interest to do that. You don't want to be in that separation meeting having these conversations. You want them to have these conversations later. You want the meeting to have dignity and have the best possible outcome.

Limit the Time Spent in a Separation Meeting

You also want to make sure that you are limiting the time you spend in a separation meeting — to a maximum of about 15 minutes. There's a saying from casino owners that's especially fitting here: "For a gambler, time is the enemy." A gambler might win and have an advantage in a short period of time, but if a gambler stays in the casino long enough, the casino will have the advantage because eventually the gambler will lose. It's the same thing in this circumstance. You must do the separation with dignity, and you must do the right thing for the individual. However, you must understand that time is your enemy and avoid talking about additional topics during a separation meeting.

It's important to do a separation correctly, but there are so many business owners who need to separate from toxic employees right now that just doing that separation is more important than thinking about how they are going to do it perfectly.

Owners and managers avoid "firing people" because they are seen as "bad guys" or "bad people" for doing this. It's so stigmatized in our society now that very few people do it often enough. We understand that. It's ruining that employee's day, and it's probably ruining yours. However, there are a lot of things you don't like doing in business that you've got to go do, and this is one of them. You'd be a maniac if you enjoyed doing it, and we don't want you to be a maniac. However, we do want you to do the tough things. Go do the hard things.

Wake-Up Call: You are not separating from toxic or underperforming staff due to the stigma of firing. It's time to move past that stigma and create a better team.

———

Well, that's it. It's time for me to separate from you. For many years, I've looked forward to the day I finished my first book, and that day is finally here. My goal is and was to stimulate thought and conversation. I've learned the hard way that I'm not always right, and at times I get it wrong. So, please take my stories, input, and experiences that I've included in this book and use them to find the answers that work best for you.

I'd love to know what you thought of the book and how it helped you. I'm not hard to find online. So, reach out and let me know what you thought.

— WADE.

WAKE-UP CALLS

———

1. Wake-Up Call: People decisions are the hardest decisions. Stop avoiding them.

2. Wake-Up Call: The work environment is one of the few places we are paid to fake trust.

3. Wake-Up Call: All partnerships eventually end, but most don't end well. (If you think your partnership is just okay, you're probably in more trouble than you think.)

4. Wake-Up Call: Friends you make at work are usually utility/fun friends. Don't expect your utility/fun friends to act like real friends.

5. Wake-Up Call: Hiring friends can create problems at work — for both you and your friends. Think through the issues ahead of time, and have a candid conversation with your friends before you hire them.

6. Wake-Up Call: Playing Superman — or trying to do everything yourself — and avoiding community are two things that are costing you personally.

7. Wake-Up Call: Do not make assumptions on the best way to hire or promote. Evaluate what makes the most sense for the position.

8. Wake-Up Call: If you don't take a break, you will break. Instead, make it a practice to have mandatory vacations.

9. Wake-Up Call: Humans are psychological, not logical. Don't treat them like logical beings.

10. Wake-Up Call: Don't think about what people will say when you are dead. Instead, think about how you will feel today. Make the right call.

11. Wake-Up Call: Don't let the daily haze block your view of annual priorities.

12. Wake Up Call: Most of us take far too little risk. After doing your due diligence, don't be afraid of taking risks and moving forward with great opportunities.

13. Wake-Up Call: You can have it all. You just can't have it all right now. Pick one path to grow and to get it all . . . eventually.

14. Wake-Up Call: If you don't have a defined hedgehog and flywheel, you will fail . . . eventually.

15. Wake-Up Call: Let your team play their positions. Don't play their positions for them.

16. Wake-Up Call: No plan is complete without a calendar.

17. Wake-Up Call: Hiring a salesperson won't solve your sales problems. (Building a better sales process will.)

18. Wake-Up Call: Be aware of the perception that's created by your business environment.

19. Wake-Up Call: As Jack Daly says, there is only one right way of selling your product or service.

20. Wake-Up Call: Don't get caught up in the emotional excitement of strategy. Leave room to execute your vision.

21. Wake-Up Call: Your company is too small to not have every employee fully engaged.

22. Wake-Up Call: As Pat Flynn said, "The riches are in the niches."

23. Wake-Up Call: Define which parts of your business must be structured and which parts can be unstructured.

24. Wake-Up Call: Be prepared for the BHAG-letdown you will feel when you achieve that ultimate goal. It's real and it happens.

25. Wake-Up Call: You are spending too much time and money on sales and too little on effective marketing.

26. Wake-Up Call: Training is good. However, execution on the training is far better.

27. Wake-Up Call: Don't just announce big ideas. Collaborate on big ideas.

28. Wake-Up Call: A rushed start will lead to rushed outcomes, but not necessarily good outcomes.

29. Wake-Up Call: You seem like a hero when you are doing someone else's work. However, you're the villain — making it difficult to sustain growth.

30. Wake-Up Call: Every company has rules. The most unfair rules are the unwritten ones.

31. Wake-Up Call: Entrepreneurs have an inclination to go it alone. If that's you, find a way to disrupt that inclination. You must build community and find support.

32. Wake-Up Call: Never get it in writing. Always put it in writing.

33. Wake-Up Call: We are all just cave painters using white boards.

34. Wake-Up Call: Vince Lombardi started training camp with these words, "Gentlemen, this is a football." Today I want to start your wake-up call with, "Readers, this is a balance sheet."

35. Wake-Up Call: Grow profit or die.

36. Wake-Up Call: You aren't prequalifying leads, and it's wasting your time.

37. Wake-Up Call: You are being rejected every day. You don't know why, and that's hurting you.

38. Wake-Up Call: You have underperforming gross profit.

39. Wake-Up Call: If you don't believe in the product or service you sell, no one else will.

40. Wake-Up Call: Dump the bonus. Start using incentive pay.

41. Wake-Up Call: You don't have enough new sales because you hired farmers, not hunters.

42. Wake-Up Call: Your funnel is only working at half strength, and you are only getting half the sales you should be getting.

43. Wake-Up Call: No one really wins without a coach. Winning is always easier with a great team!

44. Wake-Up Call: The only way to get your team to fight their human nature is to start changing yours.

45. Wake-Up Call: If you set the expectations without input, you will receive substandard performance from your team.

46. Wake-Up Call: Every leadership team has at least one underperforming member. It's time to upgrade your team.

47. Wake-Up Call: Entrepreneurs chase recognition at the cost of profit. Avoid the seduction of awards, and enjoy the ones you had no idea you were winning.

48. Wake-Up Call: Most businesses plateau. Do you know how to climb higher?

49. Wake-Up Call: Most companies do not fully onboard staff well. Create a process that helps the new employee to become a productive member of the team.

50. Wake-Up Call: Generational differences are real; pretending they are not only makes them worse.

51. Wake-Up Call: We all have problem areas in our management of people, and not correcting them is the biggest problem.

52. Wake-Up Call: You erode trust and communication when you give lazy responses to questions. Be specific on your feedback.

53. Wake-Up Call: Stop making mentorship complicated. Start a simple program today, and watch it succeed.

54. Wake-Up Call: Very few founder entrepreneurs have the ability to grow past $10 million in revenue. Far less have the ability to grow past $100 million. Assume you can't — without help.

55. Wake-Up Call: Listen to Jim Collins's question: You may have the right people on the bus, but are they in the right seats?

56. Wake-Up Call: It's not just culture. It is important to transfer culture to the frontline staff.

57. Wake-Up Call: You are walking past broken windows in your business every day and accepting them. It's time to be serious about excellence and clean up your company.

58. Wake-Up Call: It may be time to give up — on the wrong things.

59. Wake-Up Call: Your board needs better prospective on the challenges of today. You need a refresh of your board members.

60. Wake-Up Call: Develop and stick to one flywheel.

61. Wake-Up Call: You are not leveraging pay for performance. It's time to change that because compensation drives behavior.

62. Wake-Up Call: Show more gratitude in your business, and do it via handwritten notes.

63. Wake-Up Call: Stop wasting your time on abusive people. It's time to let them go.

64. Wake-Up Call: You are not separating from toxic or underperforming staff due to the stigma of firing. It's time to move past that stigma and create a better team.

NOTES

2. Those Terrifying Situations When You Have to Tell a Colleague, "I Don't Trust You"

1. Lencioni, Patrick, and Charles Stransky. *The Five Dysfunctions of a Team.* (Random House, Inc, 2002).
2. Covey, Stephen M. R. *The Speed of Trust: Why Trust Is the Ultimate Determinate of Success or Failure in Your Relationships, Career and Life.* (Simon & Schuster, 2006).

4. Aristotle's Three Kinds of Friends, and How They Impact Your Business

1. "The Internet Classics Archive: Nicomachean Ethics by Aristotle." *The Internet Classics Archive | Nicomachean Ethics by Aristotle,* classics.mit.edu/Aristotle/nicomachaen.8.viii.html.

6. How to Create the First Team Without Managers

1. Hamel, Gary, and Michele Zanini. "The End of Bureaucracy." *Harvard Business Review,* November–December 2018, hbr.org/2018/11/the-end-of-bureaucracy.
2. Hamel, Gary, and Michele Zanini. *Humanocracy: Creating Organizations as Amazing as the People inside Them.* (Harvard Business Review Press, 2020).
3. Hamel and Zanini, *Humanocracy,* 199.
4. Collins, James C., and Morten T. Hansen. *Great by Choice: Uncertainty, Chaos, and Luck: Why Some Thrive despite Them All.* (HarperCollins Publishers, 2011), 69–98.
5. Collins, James C. *Turning the Flywheel: A Monograph to Accompany Good to Great.* (HarperCollins Publishers, 2019).

8. Rules for Staycation

1. Stephen Covey, James Collins, and Sean Covey, *The 7 Habits of Highly Effective People: Powerful Lessons in Personal Change.* (Simon & Schuster, 2020).

14. My Guilty Pleasure

1. Lazarte, Brian David and James Lee Hernandez, directors. *McMillion$*. HBO, 2020.
2. Collins, James C. and Morten T. Hansen. *Great by Choice*. (Random House Business Book, 2011), 186.
3. Collins, James C. *Good to Great: Why Some Companies Make the Leap ... and Others Don't*. (HarperCollins, 2009).
4. Collins, *Good to Great*, 215–216.

15. Work on Your Business, Not in It

1. Gerber, Michael E. *The E-Myth: Why Most Businesses Don't Work and What to Do about It*. (HarperCollins, 2012).
2. Gerber, Michael E. *The E-Myth Revisited: Why Most Small Businesses Don't Work and What to Do about It*. (HarperCollins, 2017).

16. Create an Annual Calendar

1. Bridges, Frances. "5 Ways to Make Smarter New Year's Resolutions." *Forbes*, Forbes Magazine, 13 Dec. 2017, www.forbes.com/sites/francesbridges/2017/12/12/5-ways-to-make-smarter-new-years-resolutions/?sh=4668059754f1.

19. Sales in Tough Times: Get the Right People Selling the Right Things in the Best Way

1. Daly, Jack. *Hyper Sales Growth: Street-Proven Systems & Processes: How to Grow Quickly & Profitably*. (ForbesBooks, 2017).
2. Daly. *Hyper Sales Growth*.

22. Verticals: You Want to Grow? Start Limiting Yourself

1. Flynn, Pat. *Will It Fly? How to Test Your Next Business Idea so You Don't Waste Your Time and Money*. (Flynndustries, 2016).

24. Be Prepared for the Post-BHAG Letdown

1. Collins, James C. *Good to Great: Why Some Companies Make the Leap ... and Others Don't*. (HarperCollins, 2009), 197–204.

28. First Things First: How You Start Anything Is Crucial to Success

1. 1983 July, Proceedings of the National Academy of Sciences of the United States of America, Volume 80, Number 14, [Part 2: Physical Sciences], "Research and Invention" by L. H. Sarett, Start Page 4572, Quote Page 4572, Column 2, [Presented at the annual meeting of the National Academy of Sciences on April 26, 1982], Published by National Academy of Sciences, Washington D.C. (JSTOR)
2. Collins, James C., and Morten T. Hansen. *Great by Choice: Uncertainty, Chaos, and Luck: Why Some Thrive despite Them All*. (HarperCollins, 2011).

30. In Your Company, Rules Are the Last Thing That Should Be Unwritten

1. Collins, James C. *Good to Great: Why Some Companies Make the Leap ... and Others Don't*. (HarperCollins, 2009).
2. Lencioni, Patrick. "Make Your Values Mean Something." *Harvard Business Review*, 1 Aug. 2014, hbr.org/2002/07/make-your-values-mean-something.

33. Whiteboarding Best Practices

1. Guggenheim, Davis, director. *Inside Bill's Brain: Decoding Bill Gates*. Netflix, 2019.
2. Clifford, Catherine. *Bill Gates Took Solo 'Think Weeks' in a Cabin in the Woods-Why It's a Great Strategy*. CNBC, 28 July 2019, www.cnbc.com/2019/07/26/bill-gates-took-solo-think-weeks-in-a-cabin-in-the-woods.html.
3. Meier, J. D. "How to Think Like Bill Gates." *Sources of Insight*, 29 July 2015, sourcesofinsight.com/how-to-think-like-bill-gates/.

34. Sharks Are in the Water: Will You Be One of Them or Their Prey?

1. Harnish, Verne. *Scaling up: How a Few Companies Make It ... and Why the Rest Don't*. (Gazelles Inc., 2015).
2. Harnish. *Scaling Up*, 219–233.
3. Harnish. *Scaling Up*, 231.
4. Harnish. *Scaling* , 231.

38. Being Paralyzed by Poor Gross Profits

1. "How Muscles Are Paralyzed during Sleep: Finding May Suggest New Treatments for Sleep Disorders." *ScienceDaily*, 17 July 2012, www.sciencedaily.com/releases/2012/07/120711131030.htm.
2. Sorvino, Chloe. *L'Oreal's Only Female CEO, the Founder of It Cosmetics, Is Leaving.* Forbes Magazine, 30 Aug. 2019, www.forbes.com/sites/chloesorvino/2019/08/29/loreals-only-female-ceo-the-founder-of-it-cosmetics-is-leaving/?sh=5708dcc1715a.

43. No One Achieves Peak Performance without a Coach

1. Stanier, Michael Bungay. *The Coaching Habit Say Less, Ask More & Change the Way You Lead Forever.* (Box of Crayons Press, 2016).
2. Schmidt, Eric, et al. *Trillion Dollar Coach: The Leadership Playbook of Silicon Valley's Bill Campbell.* (John Murray, 2020), 72.

44. How to Conquer Human Nature's War against Achievement

1. Goldsmith, Marshall. *What Got You Here Won't Get You There.* (Hachette Books, 2007).

45. No, Don't Set Expectations for Your Employees without Engaging Them First

1. Sorenson, Susan. "How Employees' Strengths Make Your Company Stronger." *Gallup.com*, Gallup, 30 Jan. 2020, https://www.gallup.com/workplace/231605/employees-strengths-company-stronger.aspx.
2. Sorenson. "How Employees' Strengths Make Your Company Stronger."

46. What to Do About Bad Leadership Teams

1. Buckingham, Marcus. *Nine Lies about Work: A FREETHINKING Leader's Guide to the Real World.* (Harvard Business Review Press, 2019).
2. Lencioni, Patrick, and Charles Stransky. *The Five Dysfunctions of a Team.* (Random House, Inc, 2002).

3. Lencioni, Patrick. *Death by Meeting: A Leadership Fable-- about Solving the Most Painful Problem in Business.* (Jossey-Bass, 2004).
4. Lencioni. *The Five Dysfunctions of a Team.*

48. Mastering the Patterns and Plateaus of Growth

1. Harnish, Verne. *Scaling up: How a Few Companies Make It ... and Why the Rest Don't.* (Gazelles Inc., 2015), 25.
2. Harnish. *Scaling Up,* 25.
3. Harnish. *Scaling Up,* 25.
4. Schawbel, Dan. "Brian Smith: How He Turned UGG into a Successful Company." *Forbes,* 17 Nov. 2014, www.forbes.com/sites/danschawbel/2014/11/17/brian-smith-how-he-turned-ugg-into-a-billion-dollar-company/?sh=22b21aac6c66.
5. Simpson, Luke. "The Popularity of UGG(Ly) Boots." *The Chipper,* 27 Mar. 2020, chschipper.com/2020/03/the-popularity-of-ugg-ly-boots/.
6. Fasanella, Allie. "A Look at the Shoes on 'OPRAH'S Favorite THINGS' List over the Years." *Footwear News,* Footwear News, 8 Aug. 2018, footwearnews.com/2017/focus/womens/oprah-winfrey-favorite-things-all-shoes-ugg-nike-452197/.
7. Simpson. "The Popularity of UGG(Ly) Boots."

53. The Mentor Dilemma

1. Service Material from the General ... - Alcoholics Anonymous." *Estimates of A. A. Groups and Members as of December 31, 2020,* https://www.aa.org/assets/en_US/smf-53_en.pdf.
2. *General Service Office Financial Overview - Alcoholics Anonymous.* https://www.aa.org/assets/en_US/en_gsofinancialinfo.pdf.
3. Stanier, Bungay Michael. *The Coaching Habit.* (Box of Crayons Press, 2016).

54. The Law of the Lid

1. Bezos, Jeff, *Email from Jeff Bezos to Employees.* Amazon, 2 Feb. 2021, www.aboutamazon.com/news/company-news/email-from-jeff-bezos-to-employees.
2. Bezos, *Email from Jeff Bezos to Employees.*
3. John Maxwell. "The Law of the Lid." *John Maxwell,* 19 July 2013, www.johnmaxwell.com/blog/the-law-of-the-lid/.

55. Who Is on Your Bus?

1. Collins, James C. *Good to Great: Why Some Companies Make the Leap ... and Others Don't.* (HarperCollins, 2009).

57. You Know the Broken Windows Theory by Heart. Now Fix Yours.

1. Vedantam, Shankar, et al. "How a Theory of Crime and Policing Was Born, and Went Terribly Wrong." *WBUR*, WBUR, 1 Nov. 2016, www.w-bur.org/npr/500104506/broken-windows-policing-and-the-origins-of-stop-and-frisk-and-how-it-went-wrong.
2. Vedantam et al. "How a Theory of Crime and Policing Was Born".
3. Frazao, Kristine, Sinclair Broadcast Group. "Former NYC Commissioner Who Helped Dramatically Decrease CRIME Weighs in on Today's Surge." *KUTV*, 23 June 2021, kutv.com/news/nation-world/former-nyc-commissioner-who-helped-dramatically-decrease-crime-weighs-in-on-todays-surge.

60. Whatever You Do, Don't Abandon the Flywheel

1. Collins, James C. *Good to Great: Why Some Companies Make the Leap ... and Others Don't.* HarperCollins, 2009.
2. Collins, James C. *Turning the Flywheel: A Monograph to Accompany Good to Great.* (HarperCollins, 2019).
3. Collins, James C. *Turning the Flywheel: A Monograph to Accompany Good to Great.* (HarperCollins, 2019).

62. How Handwritten Notes Can Impact Your Business

1. Sturt, David. "The Easiest Thing You Can Do to Be a Great Boss." *Harvard Business Review*, 30 Nov. 2017, hbr.org/2015/11/the-easiest-thing-you-can-do-to-be-a-great-boss.
2. Collins, James C. *Good to Great: Why Some Companies Make the Leap ... and Others Don't.* (HarperCollins, 2009).

ABOUT AUTHOR

I am an executive advisor and Scaling Up coach at Red Wagon Advisors. I help mid-market companies as they scale into industry-dominating businesses.

I split my time between Red Wagon and my next tech start-up, Redegades.

My career spans over 20 years of entrepreneurship and startups. Leadership and governance have been my primary roles, and the companies I have started have had a strong focus on technology. I have spent over a decade creating and managing startups. I consider myself a digital native, coach, mentor, and innovator. I am a proud member of Generation X and my life purpose is to build teams.

I serve as president of Entrepreneurs' Organization (EO) West Michigan. I'm also a YPO international council member and an active leader on the local and regional boards.

The most recent startup that I successfully exited grew from 5 employees in 2006 to over 80 employees and $36 million in revenue in 2017. This company was listed as one of the fastest growing companies in America six years in a row by Inc. 5000.

In 2015, I was honored to be named Alumnus of the Year by Cornerstone University.

While building my businesses, I learned that nothing is more important than family. I am thankful for the support of my beautiful and accomplished wife, Alicia, and our four children — Ethan, Elijah, Ian, and Elora. Spending time with them is a priority to me, and even though they are adults, my wife, Alicia, and I still enjoy taking our family to Disney and Yosemite.

———

I would be very honored if you would leave a review on Amazon.

ALSO BY WADE W. WYANT

Coming Soon:

Targeted: Protecting Your Family from Cybersecurity and Privacy Threats

Use this book to learn how to protect your family by implementing Redegades' 7 levels of maturity to improve you cybersecurity.

Made in the USA
Monee, IL
30 December 2021

87578791R00164